AN INT
VHF/UHF F

Other Titles of Interest

AN INTRODUCTION TO
VHF/UHF FOR RADIO AMATEURS

by

I. D. POOLE
B.Sc.(Eng.), C.Eng., M.I.E.E., G3YWX

BERNARD BABANI (publishing) LTD
THE GRAMPIANS
SHEPHERDS BUSH ROAD
LONDON W6 7NF
ENGLAND

Please Note

Although every care has been taken with the production of this book to ensure that any projects, designs, modifications and/or programs etc. contained herewith, operate in a correct and safe manner and also that any components specified are normally available in Great Britain, the Publishers do not accept responsibility in any way for the failure, including fault in design, of any project, design, modification or program to work correctly or to cause damage to any other equipment that it may be connected to or used in conjunction with, or in respect of any other damage or injury that may be so caused, nor do the Publishers accept responsibility in any way for the failure to obtain specified components.

Notice is also given that if equipment that is still under warranty is modified in any way or used or connected with home-built equipment then that warranty may be void.

© 1990 BERNARD BABANI (publishing) LTD

First Published — April 1990

British Library Cataloguing in Publication Data
Poole, Ian
    An introduction to VHF/UHF for radio amateurs.
    1. Amateur radio communication
    I. Title
    621.38416

ISBN 0 85934 226 3

Printed and bound in Great Britain by Cox & Wyman Ltd, Reading

Contents

Chapter 1

INTRODUCTION TO THE VHF AND
UHF BANDS

Amateur radio is often associated with the HF or high frequency bands below 30 MHz. In fact the popular image of the hobby projected by the media nearly always focuses on operation on these bands. However, the area where there is probably more activity and growth is actually in the VHF (very high frequency) and UHF (ultra high frequency) portions of the spectrum which lie between 30 and 3000 MHz. Here there are a number of bands which present a new and totally different challenge both in terms of construction and operating. On top of this the wide section of the spectrum encompassed by these bands means that there is a tremendous amount of variety in the bands themselves. All of this means that there is plenty of scope to stimulate the interest of any licensed radio amateur or short wave listener.

The Radio Spectrum
The radio spectrum covers a very wide part of the electromagnetic spectrum. It extends from a few kilohertz or below up to many thousands of megahertz. At the low end there are stations which regularly operate on frequencies below 50 kHz. In fact there is a standard frequency transmission on 60 kHz from MSF at Rugby in England. Then at the other end of the spectrum semiconductors are being developed to operate with improved noise performances or to give higher powers at frequencies over 100 GHz (100,000 MHz).

As the radio spectrum is so wide it is split up into various sections and given designations as shown in Figure 1.1. Within the various sections are contained many familiar radio bands. For example, the MF section contains the popular medium wave broadcast band as well as ship to shore or maritime radio services and other transmissions. The HF bands are renowned for their long distance communications using the ionosphere. Amateurs and broadcasters, amongst many other users, have

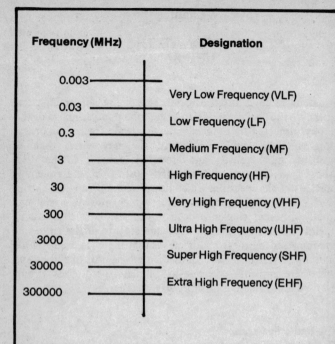

Frequency (MHz)	Designation
0.003	Very Low Frequency (VLF)
0.03	Low Frequency (LF)
0.3	Medium Frequency (MF)
3	High Frequency (HF)
30	Very High Frequency (VHF)
300	Ultra High Frequency (UHF)
3000	Super High Frequency (SHF)
30000	Extra High Frequency (EHF)
300000	

Figure 1.1 Designation of the radio spectrum.

allocations here and it is possible to hear stations from all over the world.

Increasing in frequency the VHF portion of the spectrum is found. It contains services like FM broadcasting, private mobile radio and the like. It also used to carry the old 405 line T.V. service in the U.K. and it is still used for similar services in some countries.

The UHF band is the next one higher in frequency. It contains the ground based television channels as well as many other services including cellular telephones and further private mobile radio networks.

In amongst all of these services there are several amateur bands. Many of them are the same for different countries, although there are a number of differences. The frequency allocations for the U.K. and the U.S.A. are given in Figure 1.2.

These bands are widely used. They offer many advantages and a large number of people devote all their operation to them.

U.K.	U.S.A.
50.00 – 52.00	50.00 – 54.00
70.00 – 70.50	——
144.00 – 146.00	144.00 – 148.00
——	222.00 – 225.00
430.00 – 440.00	420.00 – 450.00
——	902.00 – 928.00
1240.00 – 1325.00	1240.00 – 1300.00
2310.00 – 2450.00	$\begin{cases} 2300.00 - 2310.00 \\ 2390.00 - 2450.00 \end{cases}$

Frequencies in Megahertz

Figure 1.2 Amateur allocations in the VHF/UHF spectrum

Advantages of the VHF/UHF Bands

The character of these bands is totally different to the HF amateur band. Their bandwidth is much wider in general which means that modes like FM and the television can be accommodated. It is also found that the atmospheric noise is very much less and this has a marked effect on receiver design. It means that on these frequencies there is far more emphasis placed on the noise performance of the front end because this is the limiting factor. Other major differences which are quickly noticed include the types of propagation available. As signals are propagated by many different means their study can be very interesting.

However, it is not just the differences which make these bands so popular. There are other considerations like the ease with which stations can be set up. The VHF/UHF bands lend themselves very well to setting up a workable station quickly and easily. For a start there is plenty of ready built equipment available. Whilst some of it is very expensive there is still a good selection of less costly equipment available. Failing this there is often a plentiful supply of used commercial radio telephone equipment which can usually be modified and pressed into service.

Aerials too, need not be a problem. At these frequencies the wavelength is comparatively short and it means that aerials can be kept to a reasonable size. This is particularly advantageous for people who live in flats or do not have access to a large garden.

Another major reason for the popularity of these bands is that in many countries there is no requirement to sit a morse test to obtain a licence. For example, in the U.K. the Class B licence, for which no morse test is required, allows access to all the amateur bands above 30 MHz.

These reasons and many more have meant that bands like 2 metres (144 MHz) and 70 cms (430 MHz) have become very popular. Most amateurs have equipment for them and they are very useful for local nets and chatting as well as for DXing and experimenting.

Chapter 2

PROPAGATION

The study of propagation is one which fascinates many people. On the VHF and UHF bands there are a large number of ways in which signals can be propagated as signals can travel much further than just the direct line of sight. Often amateurs can make good use of these propagation modes and make contacts over hundreds and sometimes even thousands of miles. Unfortunately some of these modes are short lived. This means that in order to make the best use of them it is worth having an idea of what causes them and when they are most likely to occur.

The Atmosphere

Signals are propagated over distances greater than the basic line of sight and this is caused by the signals being reflected and refracted by different sections of the atmosphere. Different modes of propagation occur in different sections of the atmosphere (see Fig. 2.1) but the two main areas of interest are the troposphere and the ionosphere because it is in these two areas where the majority of the reflection and refraction occurs.

Of these two, the ionosphere is probably the one which springs to mind first of all. It stretches from about 100 kilometres to 400 kilometres in altitude. It contains the familiar E and F layers of ionisation which are responsible for propagation of signals over long distances on the HF bands and occasionally on the lower frequencies in the VHF portion of the spectrum.

There are also other effects which occur in this portion of the spectrum which are of interest to the VHF/UHF enthusiast. It is here that the effects of meteors, temporary areas of high intensity ionisation in the E layer (Sporadic E) and aurora are noticed.

It is interesting to note that the propagation which is due to effects in the ionosphere is usually very dependent on influences outside the atmosphere. For example, the condition of

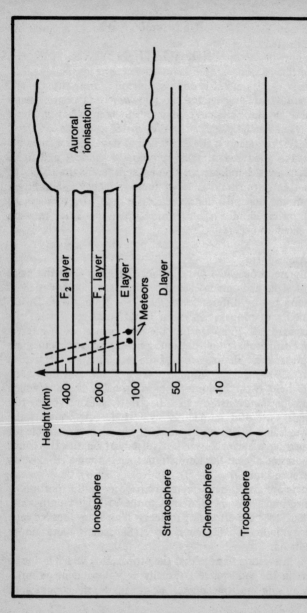

Figure 2.1 The earth's atmosphere with the ionised layers.

the E and F layers is often a result of solar activity, as are auroral effects.

Below this in the stratosphere is the D layer. The main effect this has is to absorb radio waves in the low and medium frequencies. Its effect is observed mainly during the day and this is why stations on the medium wave and above can be heard at greater distances at night. However, it has no effect on VHF and UHF signals.

The other area responsible for propagation is the troposphere. This area extends from ground level up to about 10 kilometres. As the signals which are reflected and refracted in this area do not reach anything like the height of those reflected in the ionosphere, distances which can be reached are usually much less. Even so it is still possible to make contacts over distances of 1000 km or more.

As the troposphere is the closest part of the atmosphere to the ground there are many links between the weather and radio conditions. Because of this it is possible to keep a good eye on the weather chart to see if there is any likelihood of an improvement in conditions.

Line of Sight
When there are no other forms of propagation available signals can be received up to distances of about fifty or a hundred miles, dependent upon the frequency in use and the equipment at either end. This is definitely not just the line of sight distance, as few stations would be able to make contacts over distances of five or ten miles if this were the case.

The reason for the improvement in distance is the change in refractive index of the air with increasing height. It is found that the air density changes with altitude, being more dense nearer the ground. This has a direct effect on the refractive index causing it to be higher nearer the ground. In turn this results in the radio waves, like light waves, being bent towards the area of highest refractive index. This is very convenient, because the radio waves tend to follow the earth's curvature, thereby extending the range over which they travel.

Tropospheric Ducting
One of the major effects which can cause a lift in band

7

conditions is known as tropospheric ducting, or tropo for short. It can be caused in a number of ways but it happens most often when an area of high pressure is covering the country. Warm air rises having been heated by the ground and this can result in the air closer to the ground being cooler than the air higher up. As cool air is more dense than warm air, it accentuates the density gradient with height. In turn this increases the change in refractive index and gives a greater degree of refraction of radio signals.

Similar conditions may also arise when a mass of warm air meets a mass of cooled air in a cold front. The warm air tends to rise over the cold air giving a sharp boundary. This mechanism does not usually last for as long as the high pressure lifts which may last for days. However, there is still enough time to make a good number of contacts.

Contacts using "tropo" can be made over quite significant distances. In many cases on bands like two metres and 70 centimetres it is possible to reach distances of 1000 kilometres or more.

Other Forms of Temperature Inversion
Lifts caused by areas of high pressure tend to be most common in summer, although they can happen at almost any time of the year. However, it is still possible to make contacts over considerable distances during the winter. This can often happen on crisp, frosty mornings.

On these mornings the lower layers of the air are cooled by the ground leaving the air higher up somewhat warmer. As with the standard "tropo" effect this gives a greater density and refractive index gradient than normal. This results in stations being heard over much greater distances than normal.

Sporadic E (Es)
This type of propagation gives spectacular openings on bands up to 144 MHz, although 220 MHz can be affected on rare occasions. When it occurs stations at distances up to 2000 kilometres can be heard just as on the HF bands.

Although not a great deal is known about the exact mechanism which causes sporadic E, it is known that it happens as a result of the formation of highly ionised clouds in the E layer. It is found that the level of ionisation steadily builds up, affecting first the lower frequency bands and then those higher up. Often people will use ten metres as an initial monitor to check the likelihood of any openings. Also people interested in two metre operation will check the VHF FM broadcast band for any sporadic E activity there.

The ionised clouds are comparatively small in size. They are generally less than 100 kilometres across, and only a few tens of metres thick. This means that the bands will only be open to a comparatively small area at any one time and beams have to be checked for the optimum heading. Things are also made a little more tricky by the fact that these ionised clouds tend to get blown about by the air currents in the upper atmosphere. Accordingly beam headings may have to be altered and the area to which the band is open can change.

The openings can be quite short. On two metres they may last for as little as a few minutes whilst longer ones can last for up to two or three hours. On the lower frequencies openings are considerably longer dependent on the band in use but there is always the possibility of it quickly fading out.

Sporadic E is confined to the summer months. On 6 metres there will be openings a couple of months either side of the middle of summer, but on two metres June is generally thought to produce the best openings with a few openings in May and July.

F Layer

Whilst propagation via the F layer is not normally associated with VHF it is sometimes possible on six metres and very occasionally on four metres. This occurs during the peak of the sunspot cycle when the ionisation in the E and F layers is highest. When this happens the ionisation can often be sufficiently intense for the F_2 layer to be able to reflect signals at 50 MHz.

With the F_2 layer at a height of 400 kilometres this can give a single hop distance of 3000 to 4000 kilometres. There is also the possibility of multi hop propagation and this gives the possibility of worldwide communication.

Aurora

The Northern Lights or Aurora Borealis are not only a spectacular sight, but they can also be an indication of the presence of a form of propagation known as aurora. It is found that during periods of high solar activity the sun emits streams of charged particles which travel out into the solar system. Sometimes they can reach the earth and enter its atmosphere. When this happens the Northern Lights can be seen and magnetic storms can occur. To accompany all of this there is a very large increase in the level of ionisation around the poles, which can reflect radio signals right up into the VHF portion of the spectrum.

The ionisation which occurs during an auroral "event" is very uneven and is constantly changing. This gives rise to two effects. The first is that a signal can take any one of a number of paths to reach the receiver and this gives multi path distortion. The second effect is caused by the changing nature of the ionisation. This gives rise to slight doppler shifts in the frequency of the signal. The combined result of these two effects is that any signal reflected by this means has a very rough and distinctive sound to it. Because of this it is best to use very narrow band modes like CW, although SSB can sometimes be used if signals are very good.

The distances which can be used vary widely because of the nature of the ionosphere, but generally the maximum is around 2000 kilometres. Sometimes the signal can be reflected normally as in Figure 2.2(a). At other times the signal will be back scattered or reflected back as shown in Figure 2.2(b). This means that beam headings will not always be directed towards the other station.

Like many other forms of propagation there are optimum times for aurora. It is most common in the months of March and September and then in the early evening around sunset. Another factor which affects the occurrence of auroral events is the sunspot cycle. It is found that their occurrence becomes more frequent about two years after a sunspot maximum.

An aurora is centred about the pole, stations further north are more likely to see them and be able to use them than stations further south. In fact stations in northern Scotland for example are likely to see many more auroras than stations

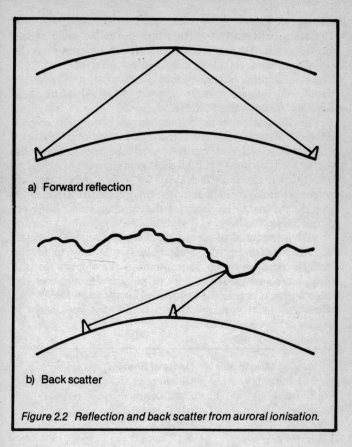

a) Forward reflection

b) Back scatter

Figure 2.2   Reflection and back scatter from auroral ionisation.

in Southern England. They will also be able to use them for longer.

Meteor Scatter

This type of propagation is possible because the earth's atmosphere is continually being bombarded by meteors of various sizes. Large meteors will leave a trail of visible ionisation and smaller ones will still leave some ionisation even though it may not be visible. The extent of the ionisation is very dependent upon the size of the meteor and it can last anywhere

11

from a second or so up to a couple of minutes. As these ionisation trails are very intense they can reflect radio signals. However, the frequency is limited with two metres generally being the highest frequency band which is affected.

These ionisation trails generally occur at an altitude of about 100 kilometres and this results in distances of up to 2000 kilometres being achieved.

Communication using meteor scatter is quite specialised. Special operating procedures and high powers combined with very directive aerials are needed. All this is needed because the ionisation trails only last for a short while and they only affect a small area. Generally high speed CW is used and contacts are often pre-arranged so that both stations can be listening on exactly the right frequency at the right time and using the correct beam heading.

Like other forms of propagation meteor scatter is subject to seasonal variations. Fortunately they are easy to predict because there are certain concentrations of meteors at particular points round the sun. As the earth passes through each one once a year it is possible to predict exactly when they occur. These "showers" are given names and they are shown in Figure 2.3.

Date of Maximum	Name of Shower
3 — 4 January	Quadrantids
22 April	April Lyrids
5 May	Eta Aquarids
7 May	Piscids
12 May	Nu Piscids
8 June	Arietids and Zeta Perseids
26 June	June Perseids
12 July	Nu Geminids
12 August	Perseids
1 November	Taurids
13 — 14 December	Geminids
22 December	Ursids

Figure 2.3 Major meteor showers

Moonbounce

Moonbounce, or EME (Earth Moon Earth), as the name implies, involves using the moon to reflect radio signals. Although it may not seem easy to do, it is found that if a large enough signal is transmitted towards the moon then a small proportion of this will be reflected and can be heard again back on earth.

There are obviously a number of difficulties to overcome when using this method of propagation. The major one is the enormous path loss which exists. This is caused by two major factors. The first is the sheer distance. The moon is about 239000 miles away and this gives a total path distance of just under half a million miles. The second factor is that the angle which the moon subtends on earth is fairly small. This means that even with a highly directional aerial array only a small portion of the transmitted power will strike the moon and then only some of this will be reflected. These and other factors give a total path loss of around 260 dB on two metres and seventy centimetres, with this figure rising with frequency. Bands below two metres could be used as the path loss is less, but the size of aerial needed to give sufficient gain would be prohibitive.

In view of these difficulties very high powers (usually greater than 500 watts) have to be used in conjunction with very sensitive receivers and high gain antennas. As a further requirement the antennas have to be capable of tracking the movement of the moon. CW is the mode which is favoured as it is easier to copy and can be used with very narrow receiver bandwidths. However, SSB has been used on occasions.

Despite these enormous difficulties this method of propagation can produce contacts over great distances. Contacts have been made over many thousands of miles which could not have been made by any other means. The only requirement being that both stations can see the moon at the same time.

Chapter 3

BANDS AND BANDPLANS

There are a wide variety of bands which are allocated to amateur radio in the VHF/UHF portion of the spectrum. At the bottom end of the scale there is six metres which has many similarities to the HF bands. At the other end of this part of the spectrum the bands have properties which make them essentially microwave bands.

Accordingly each band has its own character. It means that for a given requirement there is often an optimum band.

6 Metres 50–52 MHz (50–54 MHz in U.S.A.)
Six metres is a particularly interesting band. It combines many of the features of a VHF band with some of those which are associated with the HF bands.

Under flat band conditions it is possible to achieve distances of 100 miles or so. Then in the summer months it is frequently affected by Sporadic E. Then at the peaks of the sun spot cycle signals can be reflected by the F_2 layer. This makes intercontinental contacts possible. On occasions contacts with the other side of the world have been made.

This band is allocated to the amateur service in a limited number of countries at the moment. In North America where there is an allocation of 4 MHz it is particularly popular. It is also becoming more popular in Europe because the decline of VHF television has enabled a frequency allocation to be given to amateurs in some countries, including the U.K.

4 Metres 70.00–70.50 MHz
This band is available in only a very few countries – U.K., Eire, Gibraltar and Cyprus are four. As a result of this there is very little in the way of commercially made amateur equipment. This means that most people use equipment which is totally home-made, or has been modified from private mobile radio units. This adds to the character of the band.

Four metres regularly produces contacts over distances of 100 miles. It is often affected by Sporadic E during the summer months, although less than six metres. Additionally the band has been known to support propagation via the F_2 layer at peaks of the sunspot cycle.

2 Metres 144–146 MHz (144–148 MHz in U.S.A.)

Two metres is a very popular band for local contacts as well as DX chasing. The band is very convenient to use because it offers certain advantages. The aerials are a reasonable size and can be accommodated on most houses and the equipment is readily available. There is a widespread network of repeaters for FM and mobile operation and until recently it was the lowest frequency band available to Class B licences in the U.K. All of these factors have contributed to its popularity.

The propagation and possibility of DX add to the interest of the band. Under flat conditions contacts can be made up to fifty miles or more depending upon the equipment being used and the location. When there is a Tropo "lift" or when there is Sporadic E it is possible to make contacts over much greater distances. For the enthusiast Aurora and Meteor Scatter provide other methods of propagation.

222–225 MHz U.S.A. Only

This band is not available in Europe but in the U.S.A. it is popular for FM use. Its character is quite similar to that of two metres in terms of propagation. However, Sporadic E is seldom experienced on this band although it has been known.

70 Centimetres 430–440 MHz (420–450 MHz in U.S.A.)

Seventy centimetres or seventy cems. is another popular band. There is a growing network of repeaters in most countries which makes it very popular amongst FM operators. Having a wider bandwidth it can accommodate more channels making it an ideal choice particularly when two metres is crowded.

Line of sight and tropospheric propagation are very similar to that found on two metres, however, Sporadic E and Meteor Scatter are not experienced on the band.

For the real enthusiast with a large aerial system there is the possibility of using Moonbounce. Two metres can be used for this mode but aerials with sufficient gain become very large. This makes 70 centimetres the lowest frequency band for which this is practicable.

23 Centimetres 1240–1325 MHz

This band is becoming more popular with the advent of commercially made equipment. Even so there are currently less stations on it than on 70 centimetres.

The band gives plenty of scope for experimentation and it is capable of producing some surprising DX when there is a lift. Location is particularly important for DXing and as a result many stations will operate portably from local high spots for this reason. It is also found that paths across the sea are better than those across the land.

13 Centimetres 2310–2450 MHz

There is little commercial equipment for this band at the moment, but it is likely that this will change before too long. Currently the band is used by a number of enthusiasts and a reasonable number of contacts can be made. During contests activity increases dramatically and, like 23 centimetres, it is possible to make contacts over surprisingly long distances.

As this band is virtually a microwave band the technology which has to be used reflects this. For example, parabolic reflector or "dish" aerials are commonly used.

Bandplans

The VHF and UHF bands serve to fulfil a large number of requirements. Not only are they used for local cross town contacts but there is a large amount of mobile operation. Then they are used by DX chasers as well as the more specialised interests like satellite communications and so forth. There are also a wide variety of modes which are used, from SSB to FM and speech to packet radio. As a result it has been found that it is necessary to split the bands into segments so that different forms of communication do not interfere with one another and operation is made easier.

Figures 3.1 to 3.4 show the different bandplans which have been devised. From them it can be seen that the bands have been split into different portions dependent upon the type of mode in use. In addition to this, sections of the bands are set aside for beacons and specialised uses like satellite communication. By splitting the bands in this manner the best use is made of the available spectrum.

50.00 – 50.02	CW only
50.02 – 50.08	CW and Beacons
50.08 – 50.10	CW only
50.10 – 51.00	Narrow band modes (CW, SSB, AM, RTTY, SSTV etc.)
50.20	SSB calling frequency
50.60	RTTY calling frequency
51.00 – 51.10	Pacific DX window (narrow band only)
51.10 – 52.00	All modes (including FM and repeaters)
52.00 – 52.10	Pacific DX window (narrow band only
52.10 – 54.00	All modes (including FM and repeaters)

Figure 3.1   Region 1   6 metre bandplan

70.000 – 70.075	Beacons
70.075 – 70.150	CW
70.150 – 70.260	SSB
70.200	SSB calling frequency
70.260 – 70.400	All modes
70.260	Mobile and calling frequency
70.300	RTTY calling frequency
70.400 – 70.500	FM
70.450	FM calling frequency

Figure 3.2 U.K. 70 MHz bandplan

144.000 – 144.150	CW only
144.000 – 144.025	Moonbounce
144.050	CW calling frequency
144.100	Meteor Scatter (CW)
144.150 – 144.500	SSB and CW
144.300	SSB calling frequency
144.400	Meteor Scatter (SSB)
144.500 – 144.845	All modes
144.500	Slow Scan TV calling frequency
144.600	RTTY
144.675	Data Modes calling frequency
144.700	Fax calling frequency
144.750	ATV calling and talkback
144.845 – 144.990	Beacons
145.000 – 145.800	FM Simplex and Repeaters
145.500 (S20)	FM calling frequency
145.800 – 146.000	Satellite Operation

Figure 3.3   Region 1   2 metre bandplan

Channels

Virtually all FM operation which takes place is channelised. It has many advantages over the "free for all" type of system employed for other modes as it gives the best usage of the available spectrum and allows for easy identification of frequencies.   In addition to this equipment designed for channelised operation can change frequency far more quickly and easily than one giving continuous tuning.   This is of particular advantage for mobile operators where easy channel changes are a necessity.

. Generally the channel spacing is 25 kHz.   This allows sufficient bandwidth for a strong signal on one channel not to interfere with a station on the next.   However, as more stations are licensed and pressure on space increases there are suggestions that a system using 12.5 kHz spacing be adopted.

The systems currently in use are shown in Figures 3.5 and 3.6. Each channel is designated a number for easy identification.   On two metres simplex ones start with the letter S,

```
431.025 – 431.450  Input for 7.6 MHz Shift Repeaters *
432.000 – 432.150  CW only
432.000 – 432.025  Moonbounce
432.050            Centre of CW Activity
432.150 – 432.500  SSB and CW
432.200            Centre of SSB Activity
432.350            Microwave talkback
432.500 – 432.800  All modes
432.500            Centre of Slow Scan TV Activity
432.600            Centre of RTTY Activity
432.675            Centre of Data Modes Activity
432.700            Centre of Fax Activity
432.800 – 432.990  Beacons
433.000 – 433.375  Output for 1.6 MHz Shift Repeaters
433.400 – 434.600  FM Simplex
434.600 – 435.000  Input for 1.6 MHz Shift Repeaters
435.000 – 438.000  Satellite Operation
438.000 – 439.050  Output for 7.6 MHz Shift Repeaters *
439.050 – 440.000  TV Operation
```

*Repeaters using 7.6 MHz shift are found only in Germany
and Switzerland. U.K. Repeaters use only 1.6 MHz.

Figure 3.4   Region 1   70 cms bandplan

whereas on seventy centimetres they begin with SU. For
example, S20 is on two metres whereas SU20 is on seventy
centimetres. Similarly repeater channels are numbered in the
same way but commence with an R on two metres or RU for
seventy centimetres. For repeater operation there are both
input and output channels, however, amateur transceivers will
automatically take account of this when set for repeater
operation. In this mode they will adopt the correct frequency
when changing from transmit to receive.

145.000	R0	
145.025	R1	
145.050	R2	
145.075	R3	
145.100	R4	REPEATER INPUTS
145.125	R5	
145.150	R6	
145.175	R7	

145.200	S8	
145.225	S9	
145.250	S10	
145.275	S11	
145.300	S12	
145.325	S13	
145.350	S14	
145.375	S15	
145.400	S16	SIMPLEX CHANNELS
145.425	S17	
145.450	S18	
145.475	S19	
145.500	S20	
145.525	S21	
145.550	S22	
145.575	S23	

145.600	R0	
145.625	R1	
145.650	R2	
145.675	R3	
145.700	R4	REPEATER OUTPUTS
145.725	R5	
145.750	R6	
145.775	R7	

Figure 3.5   Two metre channel designation

433.000	RB0	
433.025	RB1	
433.050	RB2	
433.075	RB3	
433.100	RB4	
433.125	RB5	
433.150	RB6	
433.175	RB7	REPEATER CHANNELS
433.200	RB8	
433.225	RB9	
433.250	RB10	
433.275	RB11	
433.300	RB12	
433.325	RB13	
433.350	RB14	
433.375	RB15	
433.400	SU16	
433.425	SU17	
433.450	SU18	
433.475	SU19	
433.500	SU20	SIMPLEX CHANNELS
433.525	SU21	
433.550	SU22	
433.575	SU23	
433.600	SU24	
434.600	RB0	
434.625	RB1	
434.650	RB2	
434.675	RB3	
434.700	RB4	
434.725	RB5	
434.750	RB6	
434.775	RB7	REPEATER CHANNELS
434.800	RB8	
434.825	RB9	
434.850	RB10	
434.875	RB11	
434.900	RB12	
434.925	RB13	
434.950	RB14	
434.975	RB15	

Figure 3.6   Seventy centimetres channel designations

Chapter 4

RECEIVERS AND TRANSMITTERS

Equipment used on the VHF and UHF bands presents many challenges to designers and constructors alike. In the receivers designed for these frequencies one of the major requirements is for a low noise front end. In addition to this the design of the local oscillator is important and many transmitters and receivers use frequency synthesisers. Many other factors are also important. For receivers their strong signal handling capacity, whilst in a transmitter the "cleanliness" of the signal is all important to avoid any undue interference to people close by.

For constructors the use of circuit techniques not found in units used on lower frequencies represents a challenge. Surface mount technology is of particular interest as it enables circuits for higher frequencies to be constructed more reliably without the problems associated with stray inductance and capacitance.

All of this means that VHF/UHF can be an experimenter's paradise. New technologies and ideas can always be tried out. Even so, there is still room for the newcomer to find his feet, build some circuits and learn more about the techniques which can be used here.

Receivers

Receivers for the VHF and UHF bands can take a variety of forms. They are almost all superhets, although up until the late 1960's super regenerative designs were quite popular amongst those wanting to experiment with less complicated receivers.

Even though superhets are standard these days, there can be quite a difference between one receiver and the next. Some may use two or even three frequency conversions whilst some for the lower frequency bands may use only one.

In order to simplify the explanation of a typical receiver the example of the single conversion block diagram shown in Figure 4.1 will be used.

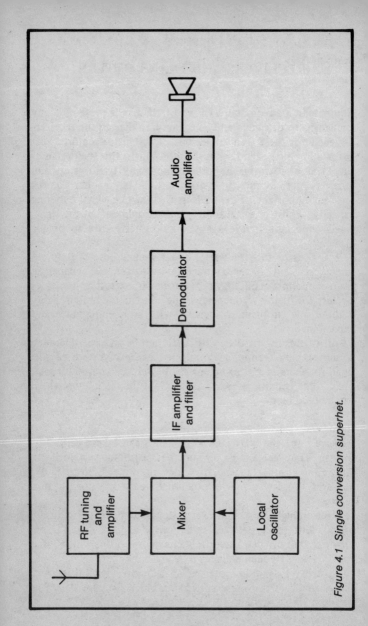

Figure 4.1 Single conversion superhet.

The signal first enters the RF amplifier stage. The purpose of this stage is two fold. One is to provide sufficient selectivity to prevent image signals reaching the IF stages. The second is to provide signal amplification before the mixer.

The noise performance of the front end stage is of the utmost importance. At frequencies in this portion of the frequency spectrum, very little atmospheric noise is received. This means that virtually all the noise heard at the output of the receiver is generated within the receiver itself. As each successive stage within the receiver will amplify noise from the previous stages, this means that noise produced in the first stage will be the most significant. This means that the design of the RF amplifier is very critical and it should be optimised to give the lowest noise.

In order to quantify the noise performance of a receiver or amplifier, a parameter called the noise figure is used. This figure can be used to specify the performance of a preamplifier or even a complete radio system.

One important factor in determining the noise figure of any system is the signal to noise ratio. This is simply the ratio of the wanted signal to the unwanted noise. Obviously if there is very little noise a good signal to noise ratio will result, but any noise which is introduced will degrade the signal to noise ratio.

Essentially the noise figure is the ratio between the signal to noise ratios at the input and output of an amplifier or receiver. It is expressed in decibels as shown below:

$$NF = 10 \log_{10} \frac{S/N \text{ at input}}{S/N \text{ at output}}$$

If the amplifier or receiver were perfect then it would not contribute any noise so that the signal to noise ratio at the input and output would be the same, giving a noise figure of 0 dB. In practice this is not so and noise figures larger than zero are always quoted. As a guide, a typical two metre preamp will have a noise figure of 1 dB or so, whilst ultra low noise versions will possess figures of less than a decibel.

Having been amplified the signal is converted down to the final intermediate frequency stages. This may be done in one or more stages. As a high intermediate frequency after the first mixer removes the unwanted image signals further away from the wanted signal, intermediate frequencies of 10.7 MHz are common. However, if a multiconversion approach is used a lower final intermediate frequency can be used.

Variable local oscillators used in tunable receivers these days normally use frequency synthesisers. If only a limited number of fixed channels are required then crystals could be used as an alternative. Ordinary variable frequency oscillators are not sufficiently stable and cannot be used.

The majority of amplification and selectivity is provided by the IF stages. Several stages are normally used to give sufficient gain and a crystal filter is generally used to give the required degree of selectivity.

The output from the IF amplifier is connected to the demodulator. As different types of demodulator are needed for different types of transmission there may be two or more different circuits which can be switched in.

For single sideband on CW product detectors with a beat frequency oscillator (b.f.o.) are used. Essentially the product detector is just a mixer and the b.f.o. beats with the incoming signal to give an audio note in the case of CW or regenerates the audio signal in the case of single sideband.

When FM is used a number of different circuits can be used. The simplest is a ratio detector as shown in Figure 4.2. However, phase locked loops are being used increasingly these days as IC's to perform this function are relatively cheap and easy to use.

Once the signal has been demodulated it can be amplified and connected to a loudspeaker, headphone or in the case of data transmissions it can be connected to the data equipment.

Preamplifiers

Not all receivers and transceivers have the desired sensitivity or noise figure. Many of the older designs which do not have the benefits of today's latest technology can be lacking in performance. This can be improved quite easily by adding a low noise preamplifier between the receiver and the aerial. As the overall "system" noise figure is governed chiefly by the first amplifier a considerable improvement can be gained

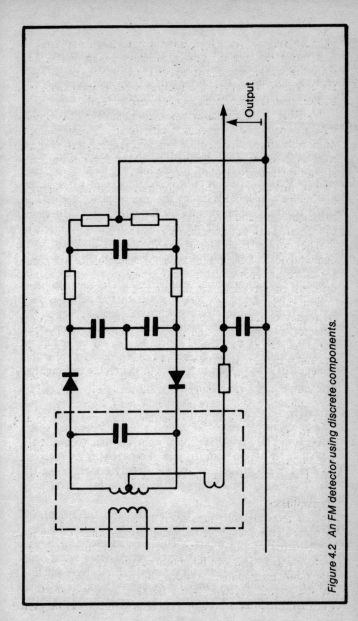

Figure 4.2 An FM detector using discrete components.

in this way.

Generally the simplest way of installing a preamplifier is to have a small outboard unit in the shack. However, the greatest benefit is obtained if the unit is mounted as near as possible to the aerial. The reason for doing this is that any loss in the feeder will degrade the overall "system" or station performance by the same amount. For example, if a receiver has a noise figure of 1 dB, but the aerial feeder has a loss of 2 dB – which is not unreasonable – then the overall station noise figure will be 3 dB. If the feeder loss occurs after the first amplifier then its effect is reduced to the extent where it can usually be ignored. This means that even a good receiver can benefit from a preamp mounted at the aerial itself. The major drawbacks of these masthead amplifiers are mainly mechanical. As they generally have to be mounted outside, their boxes have to be weatherproof. Also provision has to be made to get power to them.

Even though preamplifiers can be very useful they also have their disadvantages. The main one is that it becomes very easy to overload the receiver when strong signals appear on the band. If this happens the performance of the receiver can be degraded – strong signals can appear to splatter up and down the band, and weak signals can be masked. To solve this problem it is always wise to be able to switch the preamplifier out of the circuit or reduce its gain.

Converters

It is not always necessary to possess a receiver designed specifically for VHF or UHF use. One approach commonly adopted is to use an ordinary HF receiver with a converter. This has the advantage that anyone already possessing an HF receiver can listen on a VHF or UHF band with comparatively little financial outlay.

The block diagram for a typical converter for 2 metres is shown in Figure 4.3. Essentially it contains a fixed frequency crystal oscillator and mixer. This enables incoming signals between 144 and 146 MHz to be converted down to the band 28 to 30 MHz, which is found on most HF receivers whether amateur band only or general coverage. Therefore a signal on 144.300 MHz on two metres would appear at 28.300 MHz

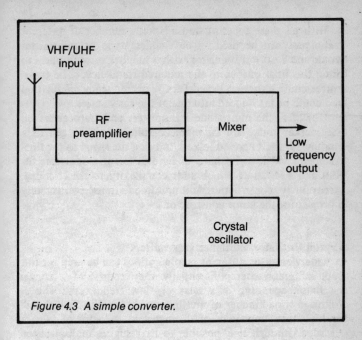

Figure 4.3 A simple converter.

on the receiver.

A converter will also contain a low noise preamplifier. This will amplify the signal before the conversion process and ensure that the system has a reasonable noise figure.

Converters are available for all of the popular bands. They follow the same basic outline, but will obviously have some changes to cater for the different frequencies. For example, a converter for use on the higher frequency bands may need some frequency multipliers to bring the oscillator output to the right frequency.

Transmitters

There is a wide variety of modes used on these bands. Channelised FM operation is popular for local nets, mobile operation and repeater work; SSB is used a lot for DX work, as is CW. Then the data modes like Amtor and packet are gaining popularity as well.

With all these types of transmission a number of different techniques can be used. The simplest type of transmitter would use a crystal oscillator with a number of multipliers to bring the final output to the required frequency. The transmitter could either be keyed for CW or frequency modulation and could be introduced into one of the early stages.

However, the multimode transmitters and transceivers on the market today are far more complicated. They generally employ synthesisers and mixers to bring the signal to the final frequency. They also have to have different modulators for SSB and FM, all of which adds complexity to the circuitry. Accordingly, construction of a multimode transceiver is rarely a project for the home constructor.

Crystal Oscillator/Multiplier Transmitters

A wide variety of different configurations can be used for this type of transmitter. Essentially they consist of a crystal oscillator operating at a relatively low frequency. This is followed by a number of multiplier stages, each of which will multiply the frequency of the signal by a factor of two or three. Although it is possible to have higher multiplication factors in each stage this is not advisable for a number of reasons. First of all the efficiency of each stage falls with the increasing multiplication factor and extra stages of amplification will be required. Secondly, filtering and tuning becomes more critical and it means that it is more difficult to select the right harmonic whilst sufficiently attenuating the unwanted ones.

Once the signal has been multiplied to the right frequency it is amplified to the right level and filtered.

In order to use the transmitter for narrow band FM, the modulation has to be applied. This is normally done at an early stage and can be carried out in a number of ways. One method is to place a varicap diode across the crystal and apply the audio voltage to it to pull its frequency slightly. This is not very satisfactory because the differing crystal characteristics will change the level of modulation from one frequency to the next. It is also found to be not very linear and this results in distortion of the audio.

30

The most favoured way is to use a phase modulator. This is far more satisfactory, but it does have a response characteristic which rises with increasing audio frequency. In order to overcome this an inverse characteristic is first applied to the audio.

The level of modulation applied at this stage need only be fairly small. This is because the amount of deviation is multiplied by the same number that the signal frequency is multiplied by. So that in order to produce 3 kHz deviation (the accepted amount for narrow band FM) at 144 MHz, only 3/18 kHz, i.e. 170 Hz need be applied if a total multiplication factor of 18 is used.

In order to illustrate how a typical transmitter may be configured an example is shown in Figure 4.4. It used an 8 MHz crystal multiplied by a factor of 18 to produce an output of 144 MHz. Other common oscillator frequencies are 12, 18 and sometimes 24 MHz. However, in each case larger amounts of frequency modulation have to be applied to achieve the correct level at the output.

Single Sideband Transmitters

Single sideband is another mode which is widely used on these frequencies. Although most sideband transmitters form part of multimode transceivers, a description of the possible block diagram of a single sideband transmitter is included to help explain the working of a multimode unit later.

The block diagram of a transmitter is shown in Figure 4.5 and it can be seen to be fairly straightforward. First of all the carrier is generated using a crystal oscillator. Generally a frequency of 10.7 MHz or sometimes 9 MHz is chosen. This is high enough to simplify the problem of removing unwanted mix products later on when the sideband signal is converted to its final frequency. It is also not so high that suitable sideband filters are not prohibitively expensive.

The signal from the carrier oscillator is applied to a balanced modulator together with the amplified and processed audio. A double sideband signal with a suppressed carrier is generated and this is then applied to a crystal filter to remove the unwanted sideband.

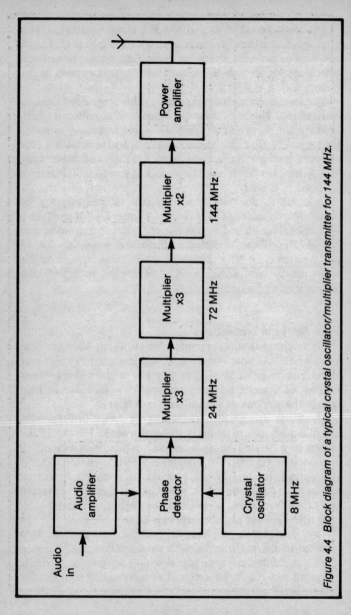

Figure 4.4 Block diagram of a typical crystal oscillator/multiplier transmitter for 144 MHz.

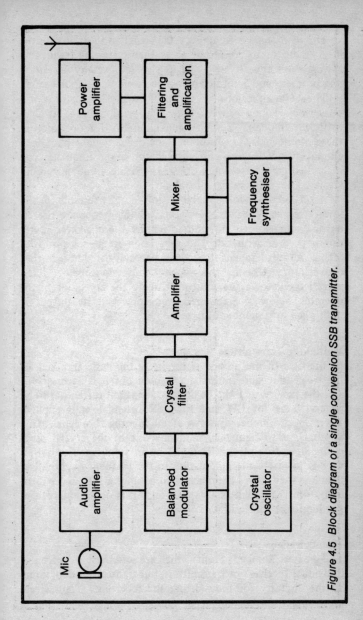

Figure 4.5 Block diagram of a single conversion SSB transmitter.

The next stage is to amplify the signal and mix it with the local oscillator to convert it to its final operating frequency. Having done this it is well filtered to remove any unwanted mix products and amplified before being presented to the aerial.

These days the local oscillator is usually in the form of a phase locked loop type of frequency synthesiser. This gives sufficient frequency stability and flexibility for operation at these frequencies. Another approach which has been employed is VXO or a crystal oscillator whose frequency can be pulled. Unfortunately straight variable frequency oscillators do not offer sufficient stability.

A single conversion approach is often quite suitable for the lower frequency bands. However, as the frequency rises it becomes increasingly difficult to remove the unwanted mixer products, even with sideband generation frequencies of 10.7 MHz. As this happens it becomes necessary to add a further conversion. Usually this second conversion uses a fixed crystal oscillator as its source. Usually the crystal oscillator operates below the required frequency and its output is multiplied up a number of times.

Multimode Transmitters
In the case of multimode transmitters the basic approach of the single sideband transmitter is used but it is necessary to add the facility of FM. To do this a constant carrier has to be generated as for CW and then the modulation is applied. There are a number of ways of modulating the signal. One approach is to frequency modulate one of the crystal oscillators used to convert the signal up in frequency. Another way is to apply the modulation to the frequency synthesiser if one is used. This approach is sometimes a little more difficult from the design aspects, but once it is operational it can produce excellent results.

Transceivers
The greatest number of units which are sold these days are not individual receivers or transmitters, but transceivers containing all the circuitry for transmitting and receiving. Transceivers are popular for a number of reasons; only a single unit is

required, the transmitter does not have to be netted onto the receiver frequency and they are cheaper.

The cost of a transceiver is less than the sum of its individual counterparts because a large portion of the circuitry can be used for both transmit and receive functions. Stages like the mixers, local oscillator, IF amplifier and so forth can all be used in both functions.

In order to make a transceiver the routing of the signal has to be changed between transmit and receive. This can be done using either relays or semiconductor switches including PIN diodes.

Frequency Synthesisers

Frequency synthesisers have already been mentioned a number of times. They are used almost universally for local oscillators in amateur receivers and transceivers today because they offer many advantages. For example, they can be very easily controlled by microprocessors, their frequency stability is excellent and they are exceedingly versatile.

Although synthesisers can take many forms, the type which has gained universal acceptance is based around the phase locked loop or PLL. A basic loop is shown in Figure 4.6 and from this it can be seen that the basic loop consists of a phase detector, voltage controlled oscillator (VCO), a loop filter and finally a reference oscillator. As the frequency stability of the loop or synthesiser is totally governed by the reference oscillator this is crystal controlled, and in professional equipment it often uses a temperature controlled oven.

The operation of the basic phase locked loop is fairly straightforward. The reference oscillator and VCO produce signals which enter the phase detector. Here an error signal is produced as a result of the phase difference between the two signals. This signal or voltage is then passed into a filter which serves several functions. It controls the loop stability, defines many of the loop characteristics and also reduces the effect of any sidebands which might be caused by any of the reference signals appearing at the VCO input (see Figure 4.7).

Once through the filter the error voltage is applied to the control input of the VCO so that the phase difference between the VCO and reference is reduced.

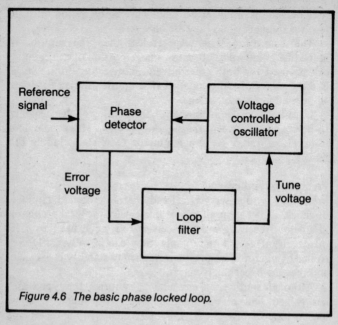

Figure 4.6 The basic phase locked loop.

When the loop has settled and is locked the error voltage will be steady and proportional to the phase difference between the reference and VCO signals. As the phase between the two signals is not changing, the frequency of the VCO is *exactly* the same as the reference.

In order to use a phase locked loop as a synthesiser a divider is placed in the loop between the VCO and phase detector. This has the effect of raising the VCO signal in proportion to the division ratio. Take the example when the divider is set to 2. The loop will reduce the phase difference between the two signals at the input of the phase detector, i.e., the frequency of both at the two phase detector inputs will be the same. The only way this can be true is if the VCO runs at twice the reference frequency. Similarly if the division ratio is 3, then the VCO will run at three times the reference frequency and so on. From this it can be seen that the oscillator will step in multiples of the reference frequency. In fact by making the divider programmable the output frequency can be

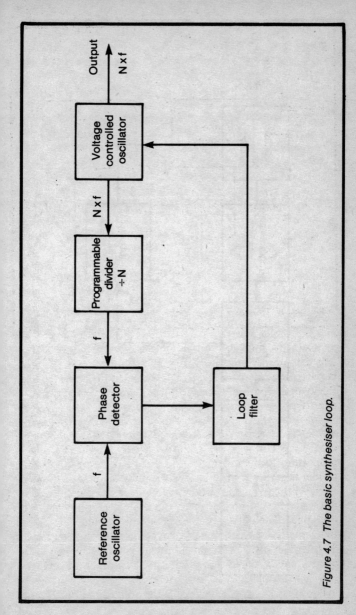

Figure 4.7 The basic synthesiser loop.

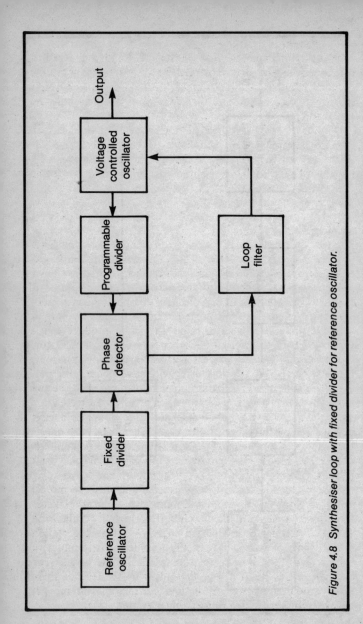

Figure 4.8 Synthesiser loop with fixed divider for reference oscillator.

easily changed.

In order to have channel spacing of 25 kHz or less the reference frequency has to be made very low. This is generally done by running the reference oscillator at a relatively high frequency, e.g., 1 MHz and then dividing it down as shown in Figure 4.8.

This is the basic synthesiser loop which is at the heart of virtually all frequency synthesisers. It can be enhanced in many ways to give more flexible operation and smaller step sizes which give almost continuous tuning and so forth. Despite all their advantages, synthesisers have one major drawback — phase noise.

Synthesiser Phase Noise

Phase noise is a form of noise which is present on all signal sources to a greater or lesser degree. Essentially it consists of noise spreading out on both sides of the main carrier as shown in Figure 4.9. Crystal oscillators are particularly clean because of the high Q of the crystals and ordinary variable frequency oscillators are generally quite acceptable. Unfortunately the way in which synthesisers operate means that they produce much higher levels of this noise than other forms of local oscillator.

Phase noise will degrade the performance of both transmitters and receivers. A transmitter with poor phase noise performance will simply "splatter" up and down the band causing interference to other local stations. A receiver is affected in a slightly different way. In fact phase noise does not always degrade the performance of a receiver. On a band with only a few signals of moderate strength it is unlikely to make much difference. However, when listening to weak signals on a band filled with strong stations it is of great importance.

The problem is caused by a process known as reciprocal mixing. Normally a station will mix with the local oscillator to produce a signal in the receiver IF passband. If the local oscillator frequency is changed slightly so that the station falls outside the passband it is still possible for it to mix with the oscillator phase noise to produce an in-band signal. The strength of this signal will be dependent on the level of phase noise produced by the synthesiser and in some instances it may be sufficiently high to mask out a wanted signal.

39

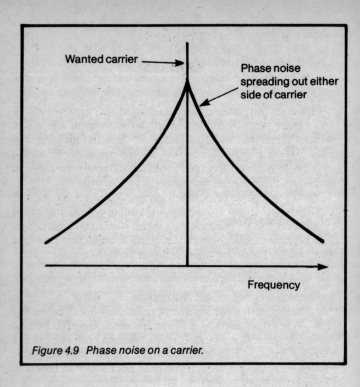

Figure 4.9 Phase noise on a carrier.

Chapter 5

AERIALS

An aerial on any radio station is a vital element in the link. A poor aerial will greatly limit the performance of the whole station regardless of the quality of the transmitting and receiving equipment. Conversely, a good aerial will make the most of it. Accordingly, time and attention spent on the aerial system is always a good investment.

The choice of aerial is not always easy and aerials come in all shapes and sizes with some designs being particularly suited to the VHF/UHF bands or to some particular application. But whatever the design of the aerial it will obey the same basic principles as any other and will perform the same function of launching an electromagnetic wave into the ether.

Electromagnetic Waves and Polarisation

The aerial radiates energy in the form of an electromagnetic wave. Like light, ultra violet rays and other forms of electromagnetic waves this energy is made up from both electric and magnetic fields. Whilst these two fields in an electromagnetic wave are inseparable they are at right angles to one another as shown in Figure 5.1.

The plane or polarisation of this wave is taken to be the same as that of the electric field. It is important because it has a bearing on a number of factors, particularly with respect to the operation of aerials. This is because an aerial will radiate a signal having a particular polarisation and similarly it will receive a signal at the maximum level when it matches the polarisation of the incoming signal.

For most aerials it is quite easy to determine the polarisation. It is simply in the same plane as the aerial itself. Accordingly a vertical aerial will radiate and receive vertically polarised signals and a horizontal aerial will radiate and receive horizontally polarised signals.

In free space once a signal has been transmitted its polarisation will remain the same. So, in order to receive signals at their maximum strength the transmitting and receiving aerials

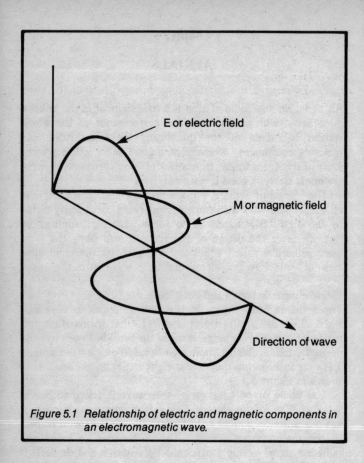

Figure 5.1 *Relationship of electric and magnetic components in an electromagnetic wave.*

must all be in the same plane. If for any reason they are at right angles they will be cross polarised and no signal will be received.

For real applications the situation is slightly different. Reflections from objects in the path of the signal will change polarisation slightly and the overall received signal will be the sum of a number of signals, each having a different polarisation and this will make matching the polarisation at each end a little less critical. Even so the overall polarisation will remain broadly the same and particularly at VHF and UHF polarisation is of great importance.

Aerial Make-up

An aerial system is made up from three parts: the radiator, the matching and coupling circuitry and the feeder which is used to connect the transmitter to the radiator.

The purpose of the radiator is self-explanatory as it serves to radiate the signal. The feeder is needed to connect a transmitter to the radiator as it may be located away from the radiating section of the aerial. One reason for this is that it is usually necessary to erect the aerial as high as possible or away from buildings or other obstructions to obtain the best results. In some instances long runs of feeder may be necessary to connect the transmitter to the radiator.

Matching and coupling arrangements are needed to ensure the correct impedance match between the feeder and the aerial. If there is a poor match between the aerial and the feeder then there will be a high level of reflected power and a high standing wave ratio. This can lead to poor levels of efficiency in the aerial system.

It is also necessary to match the output impedance of the transmitter to the feeder in order to achieve maximum efficiency.

To achieve this, the final stage of a transmitter includes a coil and capacitor network to accurately match its output to the feeder.

In order to avoid having to re-adjust transmitters each time they are connected to a different aerial system a standard impedance of 50 ohms is used. Therefore all aerials, transmitters and feeders are designed to be 50 ohms. However, care should be taken when choosing feeders as domestic television coaxial feeders do not conform to this and have an impedance of 75 ohms. Also some coax lines used for computer systems have unusual impedances.

Feeders

Feeders or transmission lines are used to transfer RF energy from one point to another, introducing only a minimal amount of loss. They do this by propagating an RF wave

43

along the length of the feeder and allowing it not to radiate. They do this by containing the electric and magnetic fields associated with the wave to the vicinity of the feeder.

There are several forms of feeder. The type which is almost universally used at these frequencies is the coaxial feeder or coax for short. It consists of an inner conductor surrounded by an insulating dielectric and covered with an outer screen or braid. In turn there is a final insulation cover to act as protection. It carries current in both the inner and outer conductors, but because they are equal and opposite all the fields are confined to within the cable and cannot radiate. As there are no fields outside the cable nearby objects do not affect its properties and it can be used to carry RF energy through many locations with little risk of them being affected.

The loss which a feeder introduces between the aerial and receiver or transmitter is of the utmost importance. Any power which it loses will reduce the efficiency of the station. In order to minimise this, low loss types of coax are almost always used at these frequencies. These coax cables are thicker than the standard types and use a semi airspaced dielectric between the inner and outer conductors. By doing this losses can be reduced to as little as 2.5 dB per 10 metres at 1000 MHz. Even so, some stations will use coax cable with even lower losses.

Another form of feeder which can be used at higher frequencies is called waveguide. Essentially it consists of a solid "pipe" which is usually rectangular in cross section, although occasionally circular ones are used.

Unlike coax it has no centre conductor, and the way it operates is different. A signal is launched or transmitted into it and as it cannot escape through the walls it travels along the waveguide.

It is found that a waveguide of particular dimensions cannot operate below a certain frequency, having what is known as a cutoff frequency. Below this no signals propagate along it. This means that a number of different sizes of waveguide are available dependent on the frequency in use. These sizes are standardised and given numbers in the form WG**. As an example, a waveguide for use between 2.60 and 3.95 GHz has internal dimensions of 72 x 34 mm and is given the designation WG10.

The main advantage of waveguide is its low loss at high frequencies compared with coax. In the case of WG10 made from aluminium it can be as low as 0.7 dB per 30 metres. Against this its cost is much higher and this means that it is not widely used in amateur projects.

Characteristic Impedance and Velocity Factor

It has already been mentioned that the maximum power transfer from a transmitter to an aerial occurs when the impedances are the same. Feeders themselves are found to have an impedance and this is of great importance when designing and erecting aerials.

The impedance of a feeder can best be demonstrated by taking the example of an infinitely long line with no losses. A signal applied to this line would propagate along it for ever and never be reflected or returned. As the energy propagating along the wire is always travelling and not stored the line would look like a pure resistor to the transmitter.

If the line was cut at a finite distance from the transmitter and the end left either open or short circuit then any signal travelling along the feeder would not be able to travel any further. In this case the only way for it to travel is to be reflected back the way it came. If then a variable resistor is connected to the end of the line some power will be dissipated in the load. As the value of the resistor is reduced it is found that more power is transferred to the load and less is reflected. Eventually a point is reached when all the power is dissipated in the resistor and none is reflected. If the value of the resistor is reduced beyond this point less power is transferred to the resistor and more becomes reflected.

The value of the resistor when no power is reflected represents the impedance of the feeder itself and it is known as the characteristic impedance. Generally coaxial cables have an impedance of 75 ohms if they are to be used for domestic television, or 50 ohms if they are for professional or amateur radio use.

In all cases, it is possible to determine the characteristic impedance of a cable. For a coaxial cable it is governed by the ratio of the diameter of the inner conductor and the inner diameter of the external braid. In addition to this it is found that the relative permittivity of the dielectric between or around the conductors also affects the impedance.

Not only does the permittivity affect the impedance but it also changes the rate at which the signal travels along the feeder. In fact the velocity is reduced by the square root of the relative permittivity. This difference in velocity is known as the velocity factor.

In many cases it can be as low as 0.66. In other words the signal travels along the cable at 0.66 times the speed of light. Whilst this may not appear to have much significance it does affect the wavelength of the signal in the feeder. This can be particularly important when it is necessary to cut resonant lengths of feeder for use as matching stubs or the like.

Voltage and Current Waveforms
In any aerial the current and voltage distribution will vary according to the position in the aerial. Some points will carry a high current and have little voltage whilst others possess a high potential but carry little current. Take as a typical example the half wave dipole aerial shown in Figure 5.2. From this it can be seen that the voltage reaches a maximum at either end and falls to zero in the middle. Conversely the current is at its maximum in the middle falling to zero at either end. From this can be imagined that the feed impedance would vary according to the position where the antenna is fed. Near either end it would be very high, whilst at the centre it would be low.

Common Types of Aerial
There are a number of standard types of aerial which have become popular in amateur circles. Most of them are available ready made from commercial manufacturers, but it is also possible to build them. Not many people do this in view of the comparatively small cost saving and the equipment and skill required to construct aerials which are robust enough to use outside.

Of the vast number of different designs for aerials which are available the most popular types are the yagi for base station

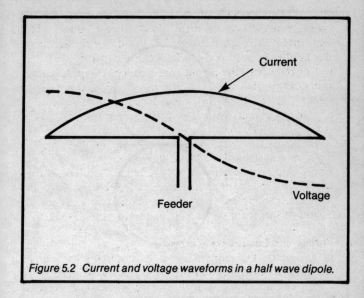

Figure 5.2 Current and voltage waveforms in a half wave dipole.

use and variants of the vertical for mobile use. Apart from these the cubical quad is seen occasionally as well as the halo. A straight dipole is not often used but it is still very important because it forms the basis for so many other types of aerial.

The Dipole
The dipole is one of the most important types of aerial. Although it is not often used at VHF and UHF in its own right, it does form the basis of a large number of other aerials which are widely used.

Although a dipole is usually thought of as a half wave aerial it can be made any number of half wavelengths. As a half wave aerial it exhibits little gain, but as the length is increased it develops lobes which tend to align progressively with the axis of the aerial as its length is increased (see Figure 5.3).

By looking at the voltage and current waveforms for the aerial it can be seen that it is fed at a point where the voltage is low and the current is high. This means that it has a low feed impedance. In free space the actual value is 78 ohms.

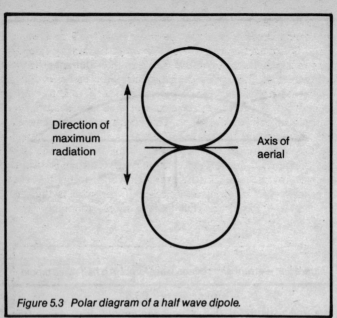

Figure 5.3 Polar diagram of a half wave dipole.

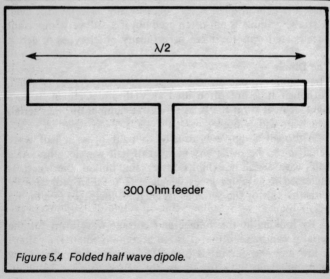

Figure 5.4 Folded half wave dipole.

48

However, when it is used with other elements in an aerial the impedance drops. In many instances it will fall to a value which is not convenient to use. In order to raise its impedance to a practicable value the dipole can be folded as shown in Figure 5.4. This raises the impedance by a factor of four.

The length of the aerial is quite critical if it is to work properly. It must be an electrical half wavelength, or multiple of half wavelengths. This length is not the same as the wavelength in free space. There are a number of reasons for this: one is called the "end effect" and is due to the fact that the aerial is not infinite. Another effect depends on the thickness of the wire. In fact it is also worth noting that the bandwidth of the aerial is increased if the wire is thicker.

A table of dipole lengths for the more commonly used bands is given in Figure 5.5.

Band	Length (ins)
4 metres	83.0
2 metres	39.4
70 cms	13.0

Figure 5.5   Dipole lengths

As with any aerial it is wise to cut the aerial slightly longer than necessary and trim it to the right length when its performance can be measured.

Halo

Even though a dipole is not very directive, it does not possess true all round radiation, having two distinct nulls along the axis of the aerial. To obtain true all round radiation verticals are used, but if a horizontally polarised signal is needed, a halo can be the solution.

As the name suggests, it is circular in shape. Essentially it is formed from a dipole which is bent round into a horizontal circle. This gives it only a slight null in the direction opposite to the gap where the two ends of the dipole nearly meet.

Yagi

In order to change the directional characteristics of the basic dipole it is possible to place other "parasitic" elements close to it. These extra elements interact with the signal being radiated in such a way that the power is either enhanced or reduced in a particular direction. Elements tend to reflect or direct the power and because of this they are given the names reflector and director.

A yagi aerial is made up as shown in Figure 5.6. The reflector behind the driven element is made about 5% longer. Only one reflector is used because any further ones do not noticeably improve the performance. One or more directors are placed in front of the driven element. The one nearest the driven element is about 5% shorter. Any further directors are made slightly shorter than this.

The spacing between the elements is not very critical. Usually it is about one-quarter to three-eighths of a wavelength, the exact spacing being chosen to adjust the feed impedance to the required value.

The addition of the parasitic elements causes the feed impedance to fall drastically. In view of this most yagi aerials use a folded dipole to bring the impedance up to a more convenient value.

Stacking Aerials

Whilst it is possible to add a large number of directors to increase the gain of an aerial, this is not always the most convenient way. As the number of directors used increases, the amount of extra gain each new one contributes falls slightly.

Another way to obtain greater gain is to use a number of aerials or arrays displaced from one another either vertically or horizontally. If the aerials are in phase then additional gain is achieved. The term used to describe this is "stacking", if one aerial is placed above another, or "baying" if they are side by side.

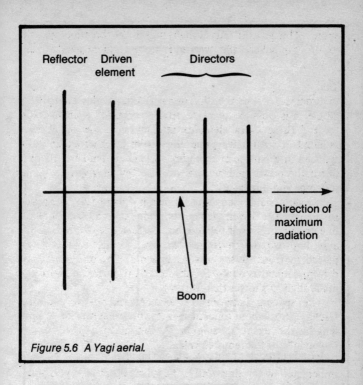

Figure 5.6 A Yagi aerial.

When aerials are used in this configuration there is an optimum distance between the two aerials. This can depend on a number of factors, but it is often around a wavelength for five-element yagis and two wavelengths for aerials over eight elements.

Cubical Quad

The cubical quad, or quad aerial is one which gained some popularity on the HF bands, but is heard of less these days. The reason is its size. Even so it has plenty to offer the VHF/UHF operator for whom the aerials are smaller and size less of a problem.

The development of the quad can best be seen by taking two dipoles stacked one above the other as shown in Figure 5.7. If their ends are bent towards one another it is found that

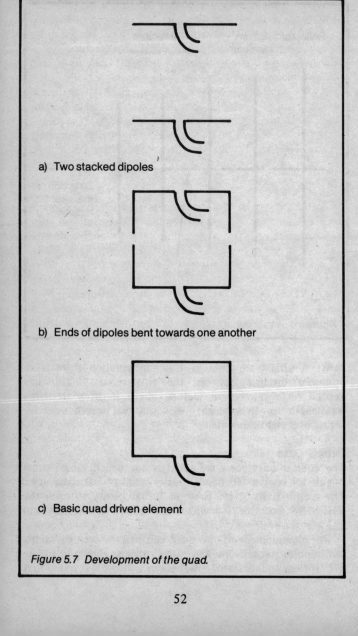

a) Two stacked dipoles

b) Ends of dipoles bent towards one another

c) Basic quad driven element

Figure 5.7 Development of the quad.

the ends of both aerials are in phase and at the same potential. The next stage is to join the ends and remove one of the feeders. This square then forms the basic element for the quad. As might be expected from the fact that it is effectively formed from two dipoles which are stacked, the basic loop itself exhibits some gain over a dipole.

Having established the basic driven element for the quad, a reflector about 5% longer can be added, as can a director about 5% shorter. Further directors can be added if required.

The spacing between the elements is not critical. Generally it is just less than a quarter of a wavelength and it can be adjusted to give the optimum match.

Verticals

Vertical aerials appear in many forms and they have become very popular with the increase in mobile FM operation. They are ideal because they offer an omnidirectional radiation pattern at a low angle (i.e., almost parallel to the ground). They are also quite easy to make and they are robust.

A vertical aerial can be likened to half a dipole in the vertical plane. The other half of the dipole is replaced by a ground plane as shown in Figure 5.8. The ground plane is ideally made up from an infinite sheet of metal. In practice it can be a number of quarter wave radials, or even a car roof. On the HF bands the ground itself is often used, however, this option is not used at VHF and above because the size of the aerials means that height is very important.

Often verticals are a quarter wavelength. However, the five-eighths of a wavelength vertical is very popular. This is because it offers gain over the quarter wavelength version by concentrating more power into a lower angle of radiation.

The Discone

The discone is an aerial which has gained popularity amongst scanner enthusiasts because of its very wide bandwidth. Often this can extend over a frequency range of ten to one.

The aerial has a very distinctive shape, as shown in Figure 5.9. From this it can be seen that it is essentially made up from a disc and a cone made of wire elements. It is because of these two shapes that it derives its name — discone.

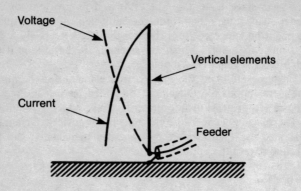

a) Current and voltage distribution in a quarter wavelength vertical

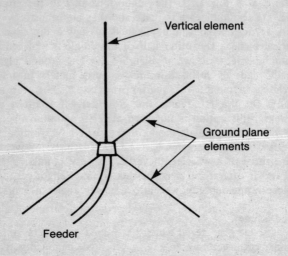

b) A quarter wave vertical with ground plane

Figure 5.8 A vertical aerial.

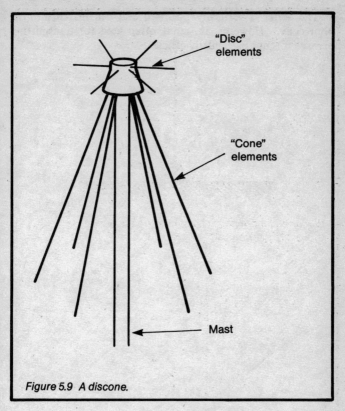

Figure 5.9 A discone.

The aerial achieves its wide bandwidth because of the conical nature of the lower elements. The number of elements which are used is not particularly critical. The more elements that are used, the better the performance because they stimulate a cone more efficiently. However, as the number of elements increase, so does the wind resistance. Normally six or eight elements are used as the optimum compromise.

The size of the aerial is governed by the lowest frequency to be used. The cone elements should be a quarter of a wavelength at the lowest frequency, whilst the diameter of the disc should be about 0.175 of a wavelength.

The aerial is vertically polarised and can match into 50 ohm coax. However, it is not often used for transmitting because it is not particularly efficient.

Chapter 6

MOBILE AND REPEATER OPERATION

Mobile operation is one aspect of amateur radio which has become increasingly popular in recent years. With the possibility of being able to operate from cars many people have been able to continue the enjoyment of their hobby whilst they are on the move.

There are many advantages associated with mobile operation. For example, it enables people to make use of time which might otherwise be wasted. It can also help remove the boredom of long distance driving. Alternatively it can just be the enjoyment of talking to other radio amateurs whilst driving along in the car.

The Growth in Mobile Operation

In the early days of amateur radio, mobile operation was not normally allowed in the U.K. However, a few experiments were permitted in the 1920's when equipment was used on board a train. Other experiments were later conducted with equipment mounted in an aircraft, but these were only isolated experiments and amateur radio was only allowed from fixed locations.

It was not until 1954 when a revision of the amateur licence took place that mobile operation was permitted on a regular basis. Even so, a supplementary licence had to be taken out in addition to the basic transmitting one. This additional licence remained a feature of mobile operation until another licence revision was performed in 1977 and the separate mobile licence was abolished.

In the 1950's and 1960's most of the mobile operation took place on the bands below 30 MHz with Top Band (160 metres) being a particular favourite. The main difficulty using these low frequency bands for mobile operation was linked with the aerials. As the natural resonant lengths were in excess of anything that could be mounted on a car the aerials had to use large loading coils. These made them both expensive and inefficient.

Towards the end of the 1960's equipment for the VHF bands and in particular 2 metres started to become available at reasonable prices. People soon discovered that VHF was far more convenient for mobile operation. In particular many aerial problems were solved because the shorter wavelengths meant that full size verticals could be made. As a result it did not take long for the surge in mobile activity at VHF and UHF to occur.

Modes for Mobile
The mode which has become most popular with mobile operators is undoubtedly FM because it has several advantages to offer. The first is that most of the flutter and other signal strength variations associated with mobile stations can be eliminated. This is possible because the receiver is only interested in the frequency variations of the signal, and the receiver IF stages can use a limiter to remove any amplitude variations. A second advantage of FM is that the receiver frequency setting is less critical than if SSB were used. This makes changing channels very much easier. However, SSB is used occasionally.

Equipment
The equipment needed for mobile operation is widely available as most amateur radio stockists will carry a good selection. Ideally any equipment should be very easy to operate and should have a minimum number of non-essential controls or facilities. It should also be compact so that it can be fitted into the car quite easily. In fact, many mobile transceivers are only slightly larger than an ordinary car radio and they can be mounted quite easily below the dashboard. A further requirement for the equipment is that it should be possible to remove it quite easily. This will enable it to be taken out of the car or hidden from view when the car is unattended and will reduce the possibility of theft.

Another requirement for mobile operation is a headset with attached microphone. Although this is not a necessity it makes operation very much easier and safer because the microphone does not have to be held.

The requirements for the aerial also need to be considered because there is a very wide choice available. Vertical aerials are used by virtually everyone, particularly on FM, although there are a few exceptions. A basic quarter wave vertical is the simplest solution, but five-eighths wavelength verticals are very popular because they give a certain amount of gain.

For mobile single sideband use, horizontal aerials are often used. This is because SSB operation takes place using horizontally polarised aerials. As a result of this a halo is the most convenient choice because it gives virtually all round radiation.

The position of the aerial on the car should also be carefully chosen. From an operational viewpoint the centre of the roof is the best. It gives a superior performance to any other position and it also reduces the possibility of there being any significant levels of radiation in the car. This can be important, particularly if high power levels are to be used.

Unfortunately the centre of the roof is not the best position if other considerations are taken into account. Holes in the centre of the roof will reduce the re-sale value of the car. To overcome this some people use magnetic mount aerials which clamp themselves to anywhere on the car without the need for holes to be drilled. However, their performance can be inferior to a conventionally mounted aerial and they also have a tendency to scratch the paintwork after a while. Another solution is to use an aerial mounted to the gutter of the car. Alternatively, the aerial can be fixed to the car in the place of the normal car aerial.

Repeaters

One of the major problems with mobile operation is that the range is often limited because the station is in a poor location. The lack of height of the aerial, and the screening effect of houses and other nearby objects often mean that signals from mobile stations are weak. To help overcome this problem a network of repeaters has been set up.

Essentially a repeater is just a unit which receives a signal on one frequency and transmits it on another. As the repeater is well sited and has a good coverage it means that any station which can transmit into the repeater will be able to be heard by any station which can hear the repeater.

How a Repeater Operates

Although repeaters are really only a form of relay station they have a number of automatically controlled functions. These functions enable them to operate in a more efficient manner and reduce the amount of spectrum pollution. This means that when operating through a repeater it is essential to have a basic knowledge of its operation so that it can be used satisfactorily.

Initially when a repeater is not in use it will not radiate a signal. In order to open the repeater up there must be a signal on its receive or input frequency. This signal must be sufficiently strong for re-transmission and it must have a short audio tone, or "tone burst" at the beginning of the transmission. The tone burst is required to ensure that noise and other unwanted signals do not activate the repeater. In addition, many repeaters check to ensure there is sufficient deviation on the signal both at initial access and later.

Once the repeater has been accessed the incoming signal will be transmitted on the output frequency. However, if the signal falls below the required level the repeater may stop the signal from being re-transmitted. Also many repeaters have a time out facility. This monitors the time a signal has been relayed and if a certain time has been exceeded then the repeater will go into a busy or time out mode and stop re-transmitting the signal. This generally occurs after about two minutes on 2 metre repeaters or five minutes on 70 centimetre ones. This facility is included to discourage people from taking too long on the repeater.

When a transmission is complete the repeater will detect that the signal has disappeared from its input. After a short delay the repeater will transmit an audio morse character as an invitation for the next station to transmit. This character is usually a "K". At this point the timers are re-set and a new transmission can start. However, this time no tone burst is required.

Once a contact has been completed and there are no further transmissions appearing on its input the repeater will close down. Before any further transmission can be made it will have to be re-opened.

In order to give the best service repeaters must have a

number of common standards. The first is the frequency of the tone burst. In the U.K. a frequency of 1750 Hz is standard. A margin of 25 Hz either way will normally access a repeater although it is wise to maintain the tone burst frequency more accurately than this.

A further standard is the channels which are used. These are outlined in Chapter 3 and from them it can be seen that there is a spacing of 600 kHz on 2 metres and 1.6 MHz on 70 centimetres between input and output frequencies. This spacing is needed to enable the repeater to transmit and receive at the same time without the transmitter interfering with the receiver.

On the Repeater

Activity on repeaters is often very high. This means that it is necessary to maintain high standards of operating and, in particular, not hold the repeater for too long. There are also a number of procedures which are special to repeater use.

The first is to note that CQ calls are not made through repeaters. Instead stations announce that they are "listening through" the repeater. This can be done quickly and it is quite sufficient to enable other stations to hear anyone who is calling and then to reply.

Once a contact has been set up it is quite possible that both stations find they can complete their contact without the use of the repeater. This is particularly true, for example, when two mobile stations are moving towards one another. If this is so then the repeater should be vacated to allow others to use it.

In addition to this, as repeaters are intended mainly for mobile stations, fixed stations should only use them when absolutely necessary and priority should be given to mobile stations.

When actually making a contact through a repeater it is necessary to be careful not to time out. To prevent this happening overs should be kept to about a minute or so. Another point is to ensure that the "K" is transmitted after each transmission. If this is not done then the repeater will assume that there has been no change in transmission and is likely to time out.

Finally, even though all repeaters follow the same basic rules, they will vary slightly. Therefore it is always wise to listen to the repeater for a while before actually using it. If this is done few problems should be encountered.

Chapter 7

DXING

DX contacts can be made by many different means. Some contacts will be made under flat conditions, whilst others may be made when there is a lift, or when there is a Sporadic E opening. Some people make contacts using more specialised methods such as meteor scatter or even moonbounce.

To enable people to use these modes successfully whilst causing the least interference to others, various operating procedures have been devised. In order to make the best use of any openings it is necessary to know what to do, and even if DX contacts are not envisaged a working knowledge of the methods used is always helpful to prevent any interference being caused to others.

In addition to the actual operating procedures there are also a number of other aspects to DXing. One is the system of defining the location of a station using "QRA locators". Another is that of collecting awards or certificates for operating challenges. All of these are integral parts of DXing on frequencies above 30 MHz.

Modes
The two most popular modes for DXing are SSB and CW. Of these sideband is more popular for general use. However, there is still a fair amount of activity on CW and it should not be ignored. In fact, contacts can often be made on CW when they would not be possible on SSB. Because of this some of the more exacting modes of operation tend to use CW more for this very reason.

Normal and Tropospheric Lift Conditions
Under normal, or flat, conditions most CQ calls are made on the "calling frequency". The idea of the calling frequency is that only one frequency has to be monitored and the amount of tuning on the band can be greatly reduced. This is a great advantage at VHF and UHF where bands are larger than they are at HF.

The band plans given in Chapter 3 define the frequencies used in the different bands and for different modes. Once contact has been made both stations agree to move to another frequency to make their contact.

As the calling frequency is used by a large number of stations, it should not be over used. CQ calls should be relatively short and if no replies are received after one or two calls a break of several minutes should be left for any other stations who may wish to use the frequency. In addition to this, once a contact is made both stations should quickly agree on a new frequency. Only when they are on their new frequency should they start their contact properly.

When a tropospheric lift occurs, activity will increase rapidly. The calling channels will become even more active and even greater care should be exercised when using it. Often in good lifts many stations will abandon the calling channel and call CQ elsewhere.

Sporadic E

Sporadic E openings are often very short lived but very spectacular. In view of this most stations will want to make as many contacts as possible. This means that good operating techniques are of the utmost importance.

The first point to note is that the calling channels are not used. There would be far too many stations wanting to use them and as conditions change very rapidly most contacts would be lost. Instead, stations make short CQ calls of around ten seconds on a free spot on the band and keep the frequency for any contacts.

In order to speed up contacts the minimum amount of information should be sent. An exchange of report and QRA locator is all that is normally required. If any more is attempted contact may be lost and other stations wanting to make contacts will become impatient.

During the course of a Sporadic E opening the area from which stations are heard will almost certainly change. Stations from one area will fade out and those from another will appear. The reason is that the ionised layers causing the reflection move in the upper atmosphere. This means that it will be necessary to be ready to adjust beam headings during the course of the opening.

Satellites

With the ever advancing frontiers of technology more "high tech" areas are becoming open to the radio amateur. This is particularly true of amateur satellite operation.

Despite the enormous cost of building a satellite and putting it into space there are a number which have been successfully launched and used by amateurs. Some of these satellites have been launched by the West but others have been launched by the Soviet Union.

In the West much of the money for these satellites comes from organisations specially set up to launch amateur satellites. In the U.S.A. the main organisation is the Radio Amateur Satellite Corporation or AMSAT for short. This corporation also has a number of affiliated groups around the world like its British offshoot AMSAT-UK.

AMSAT has launched a number of satellites. They are all called Oscar, short for Orbital Satellite Carrying Amateur Radio, and they are given a number to identify the individual satellite.

All communications satellites operate in basically the same way whether they are for commercial or amateur purposes. They contain what is called a transponder. This item receives signals in one band of frequencies and then re-transmits them in another band. This means that when transmitting to the satellite, frequencies in the "uplink" band must be used, whilst signals are received in the "downlink" band. Accordingly it is possible to check your own signal is passing through the satellite by transmitting in the uplink band whilst simultaneously listening on the corresponding downlink frequency.

The frequency bands for amateur satellites are chosen to fall within the internationally agreed satellite sub-bands within the amateur bands. For example, a Russian satellite RS8 used an uplink frequency of 145.96 to 146.00 and a downlink band of 29.46 to 29.50.

Owing to the fact that amateur satellites are in a low non-geostationary orbit they move across the sky. This means that it is necessary to know when the satellites will be within range. As a result the various satellite organisations issue data about the orbits of the satellites. In addition to this they carry beacons to indicate when they are in range.

Once in range the satellite can be used. Comparatively little power is needed and indeed too much power must be avoided as it will overload the satellite and prevent others using it. The effective radiated power (erp) must be less than 50 watts. Fortunately it is a simple matter to calculate the erp, it is just the power presented to the aerial times its gain.

When using a satellite the time is limited to a maximum of just over half an hour. Bearing this in mind CQ calls are kept short and contacts often consist of just the callsigns and reports. In spite of this there is no reason why longer contacts should not be made.

Another point to be noted is that the satellite will move across the sky, quite rapidly in some cases. As a result of this it will be necessary to periodically change the beam heading and sometimes the elevation. In fact, some people use computers to control their aerials. This makes accurate control of both azimuth and elevation possible all the time.

Meteor Scatter
Most of the meteor scatter operation takes place on two metres. It is the highest frequency amateur band which supports this mode of propagation and it is possible to use very high gain aerials. However, some operation does take place on the lower frequency bands in the VHF spectrum, but it is very much less common.

In order to make contacts using meteor scatter very sophisticated operating procedures have been adopted. This is because of the very intermittent nature of the propagation. It is also normal for contacts to be pre-arranged as this allows the exact frequencies and beam headings to be set before the contact making the change of a contact much greater. Even so, a few contacts which are not pre-arranged are made.

Contacts generally start on the hour. The first station to transmit is the most westerly one, it calls for a preset period of time (five minutes on CW or one minute on SSB). Then each station transmits and receives in alternate periods.

During the course of the contact the information exchanged is cut to an absolute minimum and sent several times. There is also a special reporting system which is used. This is quite similar to the standard readability and strength reporting system used for normal operating.

To make meteor scatter contacts some special equipment is needed. A good overall system noise figure is required (better than 2 dB) as well as a high gain aerial. Then the transmitter needs to be capable of delivering about 100 watts or more, although contacts have been made on much less.

Next, an accurate frequency measurement system is required so that the transmit and receive frequencies can be determined to within 200 Hz. Another requirement is an accurate clock so that transmit and receive times can be synchronised. Finally if CW is to be used a memory keyer and variable speed tape recorder are needed. They are required because speeds of at least 80 words per minute have to be used to ensure that contacts can be made.

Although extra equipment is needed for meteor scatter and different operating techniques are used it can be a very rewarding mode. It can often produce contacts over long distances when no other method is possible at VHF.

QRA Locators

One feature of VHF/UHF operating is the practice of using a QRA locator system. It has been developed to enable stations to be able to give a relatively accurate indication of their location without the need to resort to full latitude and longitude readings each time.

The system which is universally used today is called the "Maidenhead" system and it is approved by the International Amateur Radio Union.

Essentially it splits the world into a matrix of main areas which occupy $20°$ of longitude and $10°$ of latitude. These squares are designated by two letters, the first referring to the longitude and the second the latitude. They start at $180°$ west and $90°$ south with the square AA and finish at $180°$ east and $90°$ north with the square RR. These are letters 1 and 2 in Figure 7.1.

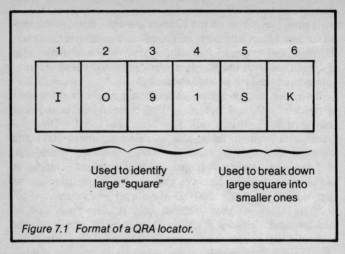

1	2	3	4	5	6
I	O	9	1	S	K

Used to identify large "square"

Used to break down large square into smaller ones

Figure 7.1   Format of a QRA locator.

These large squares are subdivided into a hundred smaller squares occupying 2° of longitude and 1° of latitude. These squares are given numeric designations starting with 00 in the south west and finishing with 99 in the north east. These two numbers occupy positions 3 and 4 in the locator.

A final subdivision is made to enable the location to be fixed even more precisely. These squares are by letter starting with AA and finishing with XX and they occupy the last two positions of the locator. The size of these squares is 5' of longitude and 2.5' of latitude.

QSL Cards and Awards

QSL cards are almost as much a part of VHF/UHF operation as they are on the HF bands. Many people will want new counties, countries or locator squares confirmed. Accordingly many people are very keen to exchange cards.

In addition to collecting QSL cards many people enjoy collecting awards and certificates. These awards can present new operating challenges, providing a goal to be attained. They are also attractive and can be mounted on the wall to decorate the shack.

A number of organisations offer awards. In the U.K. the R.S.G.B. offer a wide range. For example, their Four Metres and Down Award is very well established. It is given for contacting a number of counties and countries. The exact number varies dependent upon the band and level of award being claimed. Another award is called the Squares Award and, as the name suggests, it is given for making contact with a number of locator squares and countries.

Chapter 8

DATA COMMUNICATIONS

There is a large and growing interest in data communications. Many people find that it offers a new and interesting aspect to the hobby because it encompasses a whole new area of technology. It is also an ideal opportunity for many people to extend their interests of computing into amateur radio because home computers lend themselves very well to this field of amateur radio.

RTTY

The first form of data communication to become popular with radio amateurs was RTTY or Radio Teletype. In fact for many years it was the only form of data communication which was available and even now with the availability of home computers and other forms of communication it is still very popular.

To many people RTTY is characterised by the large and noisy teleprinters or Teletypes which were used. The most famous was the Creed Model 7 which was virtually the standard piece of equipment used by amateurs and was widely available on the surplus market. Today computers have become more widely used as they are smaller, quieter and generally more convenient.

How RTTY Works

Like any form of digital communication the characters which are to be transmitted are coded into a digital form. A standard code called the Murray Code consisting of 5 bits is used and this is shown in Figure 8.1.

As a result of the fact that only a 5 bit code is used there are only 32 different combinations which can be generated. However, there are in excess of this number of characters which are needed. The problem is overcome by using two sets of characters, one called letter case and the other called figure case. The system operates by changing between the two

71

cases by using one code or character to change to figure case and another to change to letter case.

In addition to the basic five bits used to send the data a further two bits known as the start and stop bits are used. They are placed at either end of each character and used to synchronise the receiving station to the transmitter.

Because of the need for synchronisation the receiving station has to operate at the same speed as the transmitter and standard data rates are adopted. The unit used to define the speed is known as the Baud and it corresponds to one bit per second. Two standard rates are used: 45 and 50 Baud.

Once the characters have been coded into a digital format they need to be transmitted. This is done by using two audio tones to represent the two digital states, i.e., one tone to represent a digital one or mark and the other to represent a zero or space.

There are two ways of transmitting these tones. The first is to modulate them directly as audio onto a carrier and this is known as audio frequency shift keying (AFSK). Normally frequency modulation is used with AFSK. The second method is to use the digital signals to change the frequency of the carrier. The receiving station then uses a beat frequency oscillator to generate the audio tones. This method of transmission is known as frequency shift keying (FSK).

Equipment for RTTY

A standard transceiver can obviously form the basis for any RTTY station. However, it should be stable, particularly if FSK is to be used. This is because any drift in the frequency of the receiver will result in a change of the audio tones and this may affect the copy. Fortunately most modern receivers are very stable because they use frequency synthesisers, but it may be a problem if older equipment is used. A second requirement is that the transmitter must be capable of operating at 100% duty cycle, i.e., with the carrier on all the time. This is not a problem for FM transmitters where a constant carrier level is maintained under normal operation. It can be a problem for SSB or CW transmitters where full power is normally only reached during speed peaks or key down

Lower Case	Upper Case	Code Element 5 (MSB)	4	3	2	1	Decimal Value
A	—	0	0	0	1	1	3
B	?	1	1	0	0	1	25
C	'	0	1	1	1	0	14
D	$ AB	0	1	0	0	1	9
E	3	0	0	0	0	1	1
F	! %	0	1	1	0	1	13
G	& @	1	1	0	1	0	26
H	£	1	0	1	0	0	20
I	8	0	0	1	1	0	6
J	' BELL	0	1	0	1	1	11
K	(	0	1	1	1	1	15
L	)	1	0	0	1	0	18
M	.	1	1	1	0	0	28
N	,	0	1	1	0	0	12
O	9	1	1	0	0	0	24
P	0	1	0	1	1	0	22
Q	1	1	0	1	1	1	23
R	4	0	1	0	1	0	10
S	BELL !	0	0	1	0	1	5
T	5	1	0	0	0	0	16
U	7	0	0	1	1	1	7
V	; =	1	1	1	1	0	30
W	2	1	0	0	1	1	19
X	/	1	1	1	0	1	29
Y	6	1	0	1	0	1	21
Z	" +	1	0	0	0	1	17
Space		0	0	1	0	0	4
Carriage Return		0	1	0	0	0	8
Line Feed		0	0	0	1	0	2
Figure Shift		1	1	0	1	1	27
Letter Shift		1	1	1	1	1	31
Blank		0	0	0	0	0	0

AB = Answer back also called WRU (who are you?)
Upper case characters may vary in some cases.
F, G, H (upper case) are often not used.

Figure 8.1 5 bit code used for RTTY

conditions. If full power is maintained for any length of time as in an RTTY transmission some transmitters may overheat. Before using a transmitter for RTTY it is necessary to check its ratings and reduce the power as necessary.

The next piece of equipment which is required is a modem (MOdulator/DEModulator). This unit is used to generate the necessary tones for the transmitter as well as converting the tones from receiver back to a digital format.

The final requirement is for a method of generating and displaying the digital signals. Old Teletypes or teleprinters are still used by many stations, however, home computers are usually a much better solution.

Packet

The other form of data transmission which has become very popular recently is packet radio and it has become particularly widespread on VHF. It has several advantages over the standard RTTY. Firstly it has a form of error checking built in so that the receiving station obtains a virtually error free copy. It also allows for several stations to use the same frequency at once without interfering with one another and it can be used in conjunction with "digipeaters" and "mailboxes" to extend its facilities.

As the name implies, a transmission is split up into several packets of data which are sent one at a time. This means that a complete message may need several packets. After each packet is sent the receiver sends an acknowledgement. Then the transmitter waits for the next clear slot on the frequency and then transmits the next packet and so on. If the frequency is clear the waiting time will be comparatively small, but as more stations use the frequency so the waiting time increases.

Each packet of information has a defined format, as shown in Figure 8.2. The flags at the beginning and end of each packet are used to provide synchronisation and they have a standard format. Following the first flag the next set of data contains address information, the callsigns of the source station, destination station and any repeaters which may be used are contained here. This means that the message can be ignored by any other station on the frequency. The next data

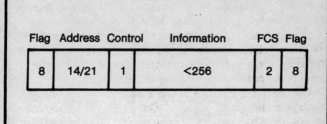

Flag	Address	Control	Information	FCS	Flag
8	14/21	1	<256	2	8

Figure 8.2 Format of a packet transmission.

to be sent is the control byte which is used to signal acknowledgements, requests to repeat the transmission and so forth. Then the message information from the keyboard is transmitted. This can be up to 256 bytes long. After this there is the FCS or frame check sequence. Its value is calculated from the data which is sent and only when the data at the receiver matches the FCS is it accepted and an acknowledgement is transmitted. Finally the terminating flag is sent. This is recognised by the receiver as the termination of the packet.

Equipment for Packet

Just as the basis of a RTTY station was formed by the transceiver, so it is with packet. As most packet transmissions are AFSK using FM almost any FM transceiver can be used.

In addition to the transceiver, other units are required so that the data can be transmitted. There are a number of ways of achieving this, however, the most common approach is to use a terminal node controller (TNC). This unit controls the transmit receive switching of the transceiver, organises the protocols associated with packet and generates the codes and tones for transmission. In addition to this it also decodes all the incoming signals from the transceiver.

Finally, a home computer or visual display unit (VDU) can be used as a display and keyboard (see Figure 8.3).

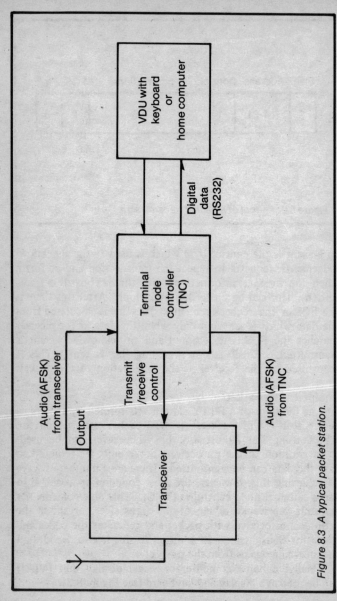

Figure 8.3 A typical packet station.

76

Digipeaters

One of the advantages of packet radio is that it can support a number of facilities which cannot easily be catered for by other forms of data communication. One of these is the use of digital repeaters or digipeaters.

Packet communication takes place on a single channel and therefore a digipeater has to transmit and receive on the same frequency unlike the FM repeaters. Digipeaters do this by receiving each packet in full and then transmitting them on to the next station. When the final station has received the message an acknowledgement is then sent back via the repeaters to the original station. This is called end to end acknowledgement.

A digipeater will not be accessed and used by every station on the frequency. The digipeater or chain of digipeaters to be used has to be specified by the sending station and this route appears in each packet which is sent. In fact, the current packet format allows for up to eight repeaters to be used. However, the route must be known in advance.

Fortunately there is no shortage of repeaters. Recent changes in the U.K. licence have enabled ordinary stations to act as repeaters. This can be done at any time whilst the station is active and will not affect its operation. All that will be noticed is that the transmitter will change over of its own accord.

The disadvantage of digipeaters is that they require end to end acknowledgement. The packet has to travel all the way to its destination before an acknowledgement is transmitted. Then the acknowledgement has to travel all the way back. If there is an error in any one link the packet has to be completely resent. If the channel is busy or the link marginal it can easily mean that the number of times a packet has to be sent before it is successful can be very high. As a result of this it is advisable to keep to known good paths and as few digipeaters as possible.

Mailboxes

Another facility which packet radio offers is that of a mailbox or Bulletin Board Systems (BBS). The idea of this facility is that a station can log onto a local mailbox. A message can be sent for another station at the same or another mailbox. This message will then be forwarded at periods of low activity from one mailbox to the next until it reaches the correct destination. Here the message will be stored until the second station logs into his mailbox and collects or reads any messages waiting for him. Obviously when sending any messages through the system it is necessary to know the correct destination mailbox.

The advantage of the mailbox system is that it is not necessary to know the route to send the information, only the destination. The reason for this is that all the necessary routing information is stored within the mailboxes themselves and they will choose the best route. However, when using the system it must be realised that messages can take a day or so to reach their destination.

Chapter 9

SCANNERS

Scanners and scanning are not strictly part of amateur radio. However, they are one aspect of the VHF/UHF arena which are becoming increasingly popular. They are freely available and can be bought relatively cheaply. As a result of this many people have bought them and are using them to listen to transmissions throughout the VHF and UHF spectrum.

Scanners are basically a form of radio designed specifically for use above frequencies of about 30 MHz. They are capable of quickly scanning a number of frequencies or channels to see if they are occupied and stopping when a signal is detected.

Using scanners it is possible to pick up a very wide variety of transmissions; from marine stations to aircraft and private users to police, they are all there.

The Law and Scanners
Before buying a scanner it is necessary to think about the legal position. The law about receiving different transmissions varies widely from one country to another. It is therefore wise to investigate the current situation.

In the United Kingdom the Wireless Telegraphy Act covers all the necessary points. It states that the public may only listen to broadcast stations, standard frequency transmissions and licensed radio amateurs. However, it is quite easy to obtain a license to pick up transmissions from weather satellites.

In spite of these restrictions scanners are widely available and are on sale quite openly. However, it is necessary to be aware of the restrictions because people have been prosecuted for listening to police transmissions.

Scanners
Scanner development has come a very long way since the first scanners were introduced. The earliest models used crystal controlled local oscillators and needed one crystal for

every channel. This placed a major restriction on these receivers because they could only monitor ten or fifteen channels.

Today's scanners use frequency synthesisers instead of crystals. This enables them to cover much wider ranges of frequencies with an almost unlimited number of channels. Even so, the coverage of most scanners is split into several ranges which usually have gaps between them. As a result it is necessary to know what frequencies will be needed before buying a scanner.

Another advantage which today's scanners possess over the earlier ones results from the use of microprocessors. By using these chips a large number of functions can be included into the receiver quite easily. For example one common facility is a large bank of memories to store regularly monitored channels. Scanners also offer the facility of programming in a band of channels which can be scanned. Another facility which some scanners have is a computer interface. This can be used to extend the facilities of the receiver quite considerably.

Size is a major feature of scanners. It is possible to buy handheld ones which are ideal for portable use. They offer many facilities including scanning, memory channels and so forth. They also usually come complete with a small pluggable flexible aerial. However, if more facilities are needed then it may be necessary to consider a larger base station unit.

Scanner Operation

A scanner will contain all the basic circuitry of any radio receiver. However, because of its mode of operation there will be additional circuits to enable it to perform all of its functions. As a result of this its controls will be different to a more conventional receiver.

The first difference to be noted will almost certainly be that a scanner possesses a keyboard. Unlike most other radios it cannot be tuned in the conventional sense and any frequencies have to be entered via the keyboard.

The keyboard will contain a large number of keys. Obviously there will be figure keys for entering frequencies but in addition to this there will be a number of other keys.

Fortunately many of these keys or functions are common between different sets even if they are made by different manufacturers.

The first of these is the Delay function. This is very useful because it determines the length of time a scanner will remain on a frequency after a transmission has ceased before it re-starts scanning.

The Enter and Memory keys are self explanatory. They are used to enter selected frequencies into the scanner memory.

The lockout facility is used to prevent particular channels from being scanned. This can be very useful because it can be used to let the scanner miss out a channel which is frequently occupied by a transmission which is not of interest. If this facility was not used the scanner would frequently stop, preventing more interesting signals from being heard.

Unlike more conventional communications receivers most scanners do not have a mode switch. Normally the scanner will automatically select the correct mode for the band in use. Only the more expensive scanners will provide external control of the mode.

Finally there is a squelch control. This is used to mute the audio output when no signals are present, and the setting of the control will determine the level at which the receiver will be muted.

The Spectrum

The frequency spectrum is put to a great variety of different uses. Broadcasters, aircraft, amateurs, CB, satellites and a whole host of other users all have to be accommodated. In order to do this the different users are allocated bands. This is done by international agreement although the final user is authorised by the government of the country. This means that there are minor variations from one country to another. However, when this happens it is done in such a way that the interference to users in other countries is minimised. One example of this was seen when the six metre band was released for amateur operation in the U.K. whilst it was still used for broadcast TV on the continent. Initially a very limited number of stations were licensed to use the band and

81

30.000	30.005	Fixed, mobile
30.005	30.01	Fixed, mobile, satellite identification, space research
30.01	35.005	Fixed, mobile
35.005	35.205	Model radio control
35.205	50.00	Fixed, mobile
50.00	52.00	Amateur
52.00	70.00	Fixed, mobile
70.00	70.50	Amateur
70.50	74.80	Fixed, mobile
74.80	75.20	Aeronautical navigation
75.20	87.50	Fixed, mobile
87.50	108.00	FM broadcast
108.00	117.975	Aeronautical radionavigation
117.975	137.00	Aeronautical mobile
137.00	138.00	Space operation, meteorological satellite, space research
138.00	144.00	Aeronautical mobile
144.00	146.00	Amateur
146.00	149.90	Fixed, mobile
149.90	150.05	Radionavigation - satellite
150.05	156.00	Fixed, mobile
156.00	162.05	Maritime mobile
162.05	173.80	Fixed, mobile
173.80	175.02	Radio microphones
175.02	272.00	Fixed, mobile
272.00	273.00	Space operation, fixed, mobile
273.00	322.00	Fixed, mobile
322.00	328.60	Radio astronomy
328.60	335.40	Aeronautical radionavigation
335.40	399.90	Fixed, mobile
399.90	400.05	Radionavigation - satellite
400.05	400.15	Standard frequency and time signal satellite

Figure 9.1 Outline of major frequency allocations between 30 and 1000 MHz

400.15	401.00	Meteorological satellites and aids, space research
401.00	402.00	Space operation and meteorological aids
402.00	406.00	Meteorological aids
406.00	406.10	Mobile satellite
406.10	430.00	Fixed, mobile
430.00	440.00	Amateur, Radio location
440.00	470.00	Fixed, mobile
470.00	582.00	Broadcasting (TV)
582.00	606.00	Fixed, mobile
606.00	854.00	Broadcast (TV)
854.00	960.00	Fixed, mobile
934.00	935.00	Citizen's Band
935.00	960.00	Fixed, mobile
960.00	1000.00	Aeronautical radionavigation

Figure 9.1 Continued

when it was released for all amateurs restrictions were imposed on aerials and power levels.

Users

An outline of the frequency allocations between 30 and 1000 MHz is given in Figure 9.1. From this it can be seen just how many different types of use there are.

Fixed, Mobile: This refers to almost any type of point to point communication. It includes the police, military, cell phones, pagers, private mobile radio and many other users.

Of these groups cell phones have received a lot of publicity recently. The two U.K. operators, Racal Vodaphone and Cellnet have found that their systems have become very popular. The main reason for this is their convenience.

Essentially cell phones are a sophisticated form of radio phone. They operate by splitting the country into small areas or cells, each covered by a base station. This base station handles all the phones which are in its cell at any one time. However, if a phone moves into another cell this will be detected and the call will be routed through the next base station. As all the base stations are linked continuous coverage can be achieved.

Another widely used form of communication is called private mobile radio (PMR). This form of communication is usually used by organisations like taxi services for maintaining contact between a base station and a number of mobile ones. PMR systems may either use a single channel simplex system or they may have split frequency operation, so it may not be possible to hear both sides of the conversation.

Another service which is offered is called a radio or car phone. This service is the predecessor to the cell phone and is not nearly as flexible. Calls can be made or received from a car but the range is limited and only some cities covered.

Paging systems also come under the umbrella of fixed, mobile. There are two main types. The first is a low power system for on-site use. The second is called wide area paging.

In general any paging system is a one way transmission. A base station transmits a signal which is picked up by the pagers but only one pager is activated because the signal carries a coded signal.

Different paging systems are able to give different levels of service. In their simplest form they just emit a "bleep" to alert the owner. Other more sophisticated systems can deliver short messages which are displayed on the receiver.

Aeronautical Mobile: This service creates a lot of interest amongst listeners. In fact people will often be seen around airports listening to the communication between the control tower and the aircraft which are taking off and landing.

Most of these communications take place in the frequency bands between 117.975 and 137.000 MHz. Operation in this band is organised so that ground stations have their own frequencies. Control towers, air traffic control and other services will have one or more sets of frequencies. The aircraft change their frequency depending upon who they need to communicate with.

Aeronautical Radio Navigation: There are a variety of radio navigation aids which are available to aircraft. They are often referred to just by their abbreviations, which may be heard in conversation on the normal aeronautical communications frequencies. The main systems are: DME (distance measuring equipment), VOR (VHF Omni Range), DVOR (Doppler VOR) and Tacan (Tactical Navigation). The Tacan system was originally set up as a military system but it is often used by commercial aircraft.

Maritime Mobile: Ship communications is another important use in the spectrum. Operation is between 156.00 and 162.05 and it is channelised, each channel being allotted a number between 1 and 88. Some of the channels are for simplex use only however, others have different transmit frequencies for ships and shore stations. This allows for full duplex operation to take place (i.e., both stations transmitting and receiving all the time).

There is a common calling and distress frequency — channel 16 on 156.8 MHz. The frequency is used in the same way as amateur calling frequencies in that initial calls are made on the frequency. Once contact has been made the stations transfer to another channel.

Space: In addition to the wide variety of land, maritime and aeronautical services, there are a growing number associated with space. Of these satellites are the most common, with meteorological ones providing the greatest interest. Fortunately it is possible to obtain a licence for this in the U.K. and although additional equipment is required to process the data and display it, many people have obtained very good and interesting results.

Apart from satellites, manned space craft use frequencies in this part of the spectrum for voice communications between their craft and earth. These transmissions can only be heard very rarely because many space craft use a comparatively low orbit and they will only be "in view" for a short time. In addition to this the frequencies they use change from time to time.

Appendix

ABBREVIATIONS AND CODES ETC.

Abbreviations

ABT	about
AGN	again
A.M.	amplitude modulation
ANT	antenna
B.C.I.	broadcast interference
BCNU	be seeing you
B.F.O.	beat frequency oscillator
BK	break
B4	before
CFM	confirm
CLD	called
C.I.O.	carrier insertion oscillator
CONDX	condition
CPI	copy
CQ	a general call
CU	see you
CUAGN	see you again
CUD	could
CW	continuous wave (often used to indicate a morse signal)
DE	from
DX	long distance
ERE	here
ES	and
FB	fine business
FER	for
F.M.	frequency modulation
FONE	telephony
GA	good afternoon
GB	goodbye
GD	good
GE	good evening
GM	good morning
GN	goodnight

GND	ground
HBREW	home brew
HI	laughter
HPE	hope
HR	here
HV	have
HW	how
LID	poor operator
LW	longwire
MOD	modulation
ND	nothing doing
NW	now
OB	old boy
OM	old man
OP	operator
OT	old timer
P.A.	power amplifier
PSE	please
R	roger (OK)
RCVD	received
RTTY	radio teletype
RX	receiver
SA	say
SED	said
SIGS	signals
SRI	sorry
S.S.B.	single sideband
STN	station
S.W.L.	short wave listener
TKS / TNX	thanks
TU	thank you
T.V.I.	television interference
TX	transmitter
U	you
UR	your, you are
VY	very
WID	with
WKD	worked
WUD	would
WX	weather

XMTR	transmitter
XTAL	crystal
XYL	wife
Z	GMT – added to the, after the time i.e., 1600Z
YL	young lady
73	best regards
88	love and kisses

Phonetic Alphabet

A	Alpha	N	November
B	Bravo	O	Oscar
C	Charlie	P	Papa
D	Delta	Q	Quebec
E	Echo	R	Romeo
F	Foxtrot	S	Sierra
G	Golf	T	Tango
H	Hotel	U	Uniform
I	India	V	Victor
J	Juliette	W	Whisky
K	Kilo	X	X-Ray
L	Lima	Y	Yankee
M	Mike	Z	Zulu

RST Code

Readability

1	Unreadable
2	Barely readable
3	Readable with difficulty
4	Readable with little difficulty
5	Totally readable

Strength

1	Faint, barely perceptible	6	Good
2	Very weak	7	Moderately strong
3	Weak	8	Strong
4	Fair	9	Very strong
5	Fairly good		

Tone

1	Extremely rough note
2	Very rough note
3	Rough note
4	Rather rough note
5	Strong ripple modulated note
6	Modulated note
7	Near d.c. note but with smooth ripple
8	Good d.c. note with a trace of ripple
9	Pure d.c. note

The Q Code

QRA   What is the name of your station?
        The name of my station is

QRB   How far are you from my station?
        I am about . . . . from your station

QRG   What is my exact frequency?
        Your exact frequency is . . . .

QRH   Does my frequency vary?
        Your frequency varies

QRI   Does my note of transmission vary?
        Your note varies

QRJ   Is my signal weak?
        Your signals are weak

QRK   What is the readability of my signal?
        The readability of your signal is . . . .

QRL   Are you busy?
        I am busy

QRM   Is there any (man made) interference?
        There is (man made) interference

QRN	Is there any atmospheric noise? There is atmospheric noise
QRO	Shall I increase my power? Increase power
QRP	Shall I reduce my power? Reduce power
QRQ	Shall I send faster? Send faster
QRS	Shall I send more slowly? Send more slowly
QRT	Shall I stop sending? Stop sending
QRU	Do you have any messages for me? I have nothing for you
QRV	Are you ready to receive? I am ready
QRZ	Who is calling me? You are being called by . . . .
QSK	Can you hear between your signals, i.e., use break in? I can hear between my signals
QSL	Can you acknowledge receipt? I acknowledge receipt
QSP	Can you relay a message? I can relay a message
QSV	Shall I send a series of V's? I will send a series of V's

QSY	Shall I change to another frequency?
	Change to another frequency
QTH	What is your location?
	My location is . . . .
QTR	What is the exact time?
	The exact time is . . . .

Index

Notes

Notes

Please note following is a list of other titles that are available in our range of Radio, Electronics and Computer books.

These should be available from all good Booksellers, Radio Component Dealers and Mail Order Companies.

However, should you experience difficulty in obtaining any title in your area, then please write directly to the Publisher enclosing payment to cover the cost of the book plus adequate postage.

If you would like a complete catalogue of our entire range of Radio, Electronics and Computer Books then please send a Stamped Addressed Envelope to:

BERNARD BABANI (publishing) LTD
THE GRAMPIANS
SHEPHERDS BUSH ROAD
LONDON W6 7NF
ENGLAND